# Garden
## Details

Decorative elements to beautify your garden

# Garden
## Details

Decorative elements for your garden

# Lynne Blundell

APPLE

First published in the UK in 2007 by
Apple Press
Sheridan House
114 Western Road
Hove
East Sussex BN3 1DD
United Kingdom

www.apple-press.com

Copyright © 2005 text, photography and design:
Lansdowne Publishing Pty Ltd
**Created and produced by Lansdowne Publishing**
sales@lanspub.com.au

Commissioned by Deborah Nixon
Text: Lynne Blundell
Photography: Leigh Clapp
Design: Robyn Latimer
Copy Editor: Susin Chow
Production: Sally Stokes and Eleanor Cant
Project Co-ordinator: Kate Merrifield

ISBN 978 1 84543 198 3

Set in Cantoria on QuarkXPress
Printed in Singapore by Tien Wah Press Pte Ltd

# Contents

# INTRODUCTION

Gardens fulfill a primitive need in humans; they allow us to leave our mark on a small piece of ground, whether that means paving a courtyard and knocking up a rough garden shed or creating an elaborate series of garden rooms complete with perennial borders and topiary shapes.

It is the decorative details that we put into our gardens, from the initial planning stage through to the final touches, that give them their own special personality and flavor. At times the vast array of choices, while exciting, can seem a little daunting. But inspiration can come from many sources and the gardens of both past and present offer you the chance to reflect on the styles and decorative effects that work best for your garden.

We have been cultivating the land and molding and changing it to make gardens of all shapes, sizes and styles since we first walked the earth. And as our numbers increase and our space becomes more limited, we continue to create gardens. In fact, if the number of gardening magazines, books and television programs that are produced is anything to go by, we are more interested in them than ever.

OPPOSITE: Sandstone stepping stones lead to the garden beyond, which is only partly revealed through the arched hedges, bringing a sense of mystery and discovery.

BELOW LEFT: An outdoor room provides a secluded area for quiet contemplation or social gatherings.

BELOW: The heavy stone table and metal chairs add a touch of elegance to this airy outdoor eating pavilion.

BOTTOM: A casual setting of teak dining furniture is the perfect complement to this tropical garden.

Gardens inspire and revitalize us. Where once we were in touch with the natural landscape and drew energy and inspiration from it, most of us now live in urban environments. This does not stop us hankering after the outdoors—it just makes our gardens even more precious, and we increasingly use them as an extension of our homes.

This outdoor room serves many purposes—it is a sanctuary from the outside world, it stimulates our senses through an interplay of color, texture and forms, and it provides a space where we can enjoy our leisure time with friends and family. In this, we seem to have come full circle. Some of the finest examples of the garden as an outdoor room date back to the ancient Romans, who perfected the use of the courtyard as part of the home. They created retreats from the demands of everyday life, complete with shady arbors, covered walkways, intricate mosaics, wall murals and ornate containers.

We have drawn inspiration from these and other early gardens. Their influences have been passed down through the centuries to find their way into contemporary gardens. The Islamic notion of the garden as a paradise on earth and a place of peaceful seclusion is just as relevant today as it was to Medieval Europeans when they developed the idea into their walled pleasure gardens. And while most of us can't replicate the scale of the grand gardens of the eighteenth century, the concepts of linear perspective and focal points still apply.

The influence of many of the great garden designers from the past is still apparent in garden styles throughout the world. Le Notre's expert use of linear perspective and grand vistas can be seen in the avenues of pleached limes that march across France, the sweeping landscapes of Capability Brown are echoed in the work of the natural garden movement, and Gertrude Jekyll's brilliant plant combinations are visible in perennial borders from Australia to northern Europe.

The clean uncluttered lines of the contemporary urban courtyard garden also owe much to the masters of minimalist gardens, the Japanese.

Contemporary gardeners and designers draw from a rich source of inspiration. A memorable feature of an historic garden or the beauty of a natural landscape can trigger an idea for a garden treatment. Or the inspiration could come from modern architecture and design, or the abstract symbolism of a Japanese stone garden.

One of the best things about creating gardens today is that we can take ideas from the past and interpret them in new ways through the use of modern materials and technology. Materials such as glass, metal, rubber and synthetics give us a much wider choice. For example, nonslip glass can be used to create transparent flooring, and metal sheeting and rubber can be combined with natural materials such as stone or timber for interesting contrasts. Streamlined materials such as stainless steel and galvanized metal put a whole new slant on the minimalist approach.

Whatever inspires you, it is the choices you make when planning your garden, from paving materials and vertical structures to the plants in your perennial border or ornamental pond, that will give it a distinctive character. These are the details that put your individual mark on your garden and help you create an outdoor space that you will enjoy for years to come.

ABOVE: Rich contrasts in texture, color and form bring vitality and depth to this contemporary courtyard. The smooth ball-shaped sculptures and river stones contrast dramatically with the spikiness of the succulents and feature plants, while the orange rendered wall is the perfect foil for the garden's highly textured materials and foliage. A metal gate with moon motif adds a touch of whimsy.

OPPOSITE: This walled European garden shows a strong Islamic influence, the pond and row of water spouts creating a tranquil atmosphere and the arched pavilion offering a welcome retreat from the summer heat.

# Style

## Influences

# STYLE INFLUENCES

Creating gardens is fundamentally about molding nature and presenting it in a form that pleases us. Human beings have been cultivating plants and creating gardens for millennia, whether for food and basic survival or for pure pleasure. Our current knowledge of plants, garden design and construction methods has been passed down through generations and across cultures. We have adopted, adapted, modified and re-created ideas from the past, with new forms evolving to suit lifestyle, climate and culture.

Up until the nineteenth century, highly structured gardens designed purely for aesthetic reasons were luxuries restricted to the very wealthy or to royalty. The gardens of today, whether public or private, large or small, still reflect many of the principles employed in creating the grand gardens of the past. Here, we look at some of the most significant influences on garden design over the centuries and how they still shape the way we construct our contemporary gardens.

Modern gardens are unlikely to slavishly follow any one of these styles, but often contain details and elements from several. Some of the current garden styles have evolved to suit specific climatic conditions. While these have also borrowed ideas and knowledge from the past, they recognize the need for flexibility in design and for understanding of local climates and plant species.

RIGHT: A strong New Mexico flavor in this colorful garden is created with the use of tiles, inlaid pebbles and vibrant blue walls.

OPPOSITE, TOP LEFT: An oriental-style water feature is given a contemporary touch with the use of metal meshing.

OPPOSITE, TOP RIGHT: The perennial border and gravel path, perfected in the 19th century by Gertrude Jekyll, is still hugely popular in gardens throughout the world.

OPPOSITE, BELOW LEFT: A mass of climbing roses in this enclosed courtyard creates a sense of abundance, typical of the cottage garden style.

OPPOSITE, BELOW RIGHT: Water features bring an element of magic to the garden. In this series of ponds each is given a distinctly different mood and style through the use of planting.

## FORMAL STYLES

### From classical Rome to inspired Islamic

Formal gardens have experienced a revival in the twenty-first century, particularly for city dwellers. The strong geometric lines, simplicity of structure, and emphasis on perspective and proportion of formal gardens adapt well to the confined spaces of city living.

Many of the principles of contemporary formal garden design can be traced back to the classical gardens of ancient Rome. We are able to see the extravagance and intricate planning of these Roman gardens in remaining ruins, especially in the perfectly preserved remains of Pompeii. In Pompeii, the townhouses were built around a series of internal garden "rooms" in which fruit trees, vegetables and herbs were grown. Murals depicting lush garden views and other scenes adorned courtyard walls, both extending the small courtyard gardens through a trompe l'oeil effect and exploring the ideal of a garden paradise.

LEFT: A small courtyard is visually extended through the skilful use of trompe l'oeil.

BELOW: A water channel with blue border incorporates the design principles first used in ancient Islamic gardens where water, the giver of life, was the central theme

From the time of the death of the prophet Mohammed in 632AD, Islam spread rapidly through central Asia, Europe and northern Africa. The followers of Islam, the Muslims, already had advanced gardening skills, and to these they added the knowledge of the cultures they encountered, particularly those of Persia, to develop sublime, intricately designed gardens according to the teachings of the Koran. Both a sensual and religious experience, the garden was a terrestrial paradise or foretaste of Heaven. Within its protective walls was a sanctuary, with cool shade, running water and an abundance of lush plants, where one could commune with the higher spirit and be removed from worldly concerns.

The traditional Islamic fourfold garden was based on a strict symbolic pattern. Fundamental to the whole concept was water—the purifier and essence of life itself. Water channels meeting at a central basin or fountain divided the garden into four sections, the number being significant to the religion. Fruit trees, roses and scented plants were contained in geometrically arranged beds, often placed below paths to create a sense of walking on a carpet of flowers and trees; pathways and contemplation platforms were made of elaborate stone work, mosaic or marble. The fourfold garden was considered a form of high art, and while there were variations due to climate and available plants, the basic layout and concept can be found throughout the Islamic world.

As more travelers explored Islamic countries, particularly the Europeans from the fifteenth century onwards, these garden design ideas and horticultural practices spread further. Today, across all cultures, many of the traditional design details of Islamic gardens are more applicable than ever. The sense of enclosure and sanctuary particularly appeals to a modern, predominantly urban society, and contemporary cityscapes lend themselves to the controlled geometry so apparent in the ancient gardens of Islam and Rome.

## Medieval seclusion and Elizabethan fragrance

Just as the gardens of Islam represented to Muslims a paradise on earth, for the Medieval Christians the enclosed garden was the "Garden of Eden." The walled garden itself represented the purity of the Virgin Mary, the rose was her special flower, red roses were the blood of martyrs, and the white Madonna lilies symbolized the Annunciation. So as well as being a place of beauty and repose, the Medieval "pleasure garden" also had elements of religious significance.

The typical Medieval *hortus conclusus*—enclosed garden—consisted of an open central lawn dotted with numerous flowers and containing a fountain. The lawn was typically surrounded by beds of scented herbs and flowers and inviting benches shaded by fruit trees or vines. Perfumed rose and vine-covered bowers were used as settings for dalliance and romance, and inspired poets and artists of the time. In the Medieval castles and abbeys, enclosed herb gardens were set within extensive grounds that contained orchards, fish-filled streams, aviaries, menageries and forests.

As Europe emerged from the Middle Ages, fragrant gardens full of herbs and flowers flourished. Patterned and knot gardens became extremely popular in Elizabethan England, with geometric designs outlined in low box hedges and clipped herbs such as lavender, rosemary, marjoram and thyme. Two kinds of knot were common: open knots filled with colored sand and gravel, and closed knots containing fragrant flowers such as wallflowers, violets, primroses and stock. Most knot gardens imitated the patterns of lacework, though grander estates often featured emblems and other intricate designs.

PAGE 16: The influence of the traditional Islamic fourfold garden is apparent in this urban courtyard, the narrow water rills bisecting the strong geometric lines of the paved area.

PAGE 17: In this Moorish-style courtyard the central water channel is accentuated with strong geometric lines and rows of brightly colored tiles. A simple waterspout and fountain is visually emphasized by the checkered pattern of blue and white tiles.

ABOVE: Knot gardens outlined with neatly clipped box hedging and filled with fragrant flowers, herbs or gravel were hugely popular in Elizabethan England. These two modern examples clearly illustrate the appeal of clipped formality combined with floral abundance.

OPPOSITE: The walled garden with its sense of seclusion is the ideal retreat from the outside world. Here, water irises thrive in a pond tucked into a quiet corner of the garden.

## Renaissance elegance

The gardens of the Italian Renaissance have had a lasting impact on modern garden designs and on the way we decorate our gardens. A time of elegance and extravagance, the Renaissance featured gardens inspired by classical garden layouts, with the emphasis on symmetry and proportion. By the fourteenth century the idea began to emerge that gardens were more than purely useful spaces or expressions of religious symbolism. Once again gardens were valued for their aesthetic appeal, and Italian nobles turned their attention to creating pleasure palaces with extensive ornamental gardens.

At first, the Italian Renaissance gardens were built on the Medieval model, constructed as an annex to the house and containing separate sections full of exotic flower species.

Over time they evolved, becoming more influenced by the ancient Roman concept of the garden as an extension of the house, with a series of interconnecting spaces or "rooms." These geometric sections were linked by a common axis with sophisticated use of linear perspective. This was emphasized by double lines of trees and bushes, architectural structures such as pergolas, and tunnels of hedges or trained vines, and ornamental features such as urns and statues were used as focal points.

BELOW: An elaborately decorated mosaic urn makes a stunning feature in this formal Italian-style garden.

OPPOSITE: The Italian Renaissance had a lasting impact on the world's gardens. These gardens clearly illustrate the key elements of classic Italian design – strong geometric lines, masterful use of linear perspective and the careful placement of decorative features such as ponds, urns and benches to emphasize focal points.

In the gardens of Renaissance Italy in the fifteenth and sixteenth centuries, the perimeters were enclosed by walls covered with trellised vegetation or by high hedges. However, by the seventeenth century the style had evolved—pergolas had been replaced by wall-like plantings of evergreens, and pencil-shaped cypresses lined the main axis and pathways.

Most of the Renaissance gardens we see today are from the later period—green architectural gardens featuring form and texture, with no evidence of the flowerbeds of the earlier Renaissance gardens—and this is widely regarded as the classical Italian style. The design features of the later Renaissance have readily adapted to the lifestyle of many contemporary urban dwellers seeking gardens that extend their living space and have a strong sense of structure and order. It is also a popular style for larger properties, where formal gardens with a geometric layout can be used close to the house and a more casual style can be adopted for the remainder of the garden.

ABOVE: This contemporary courtyard combines strong classical lines with modern flair. The slate topped seat doubles as a water feature, its shape repeated in the clipped hedge nearby.

RIGHT: An avenue of pencil-shaped conifers provides dramatic vertical emphasis to the low lines of the gravel-filled parterres.

## French formality

The classical sense of order was taken to the extreme by the French in their elaborate parterres of green scrollwork, clipped living walls and fine topiary, seen at its peak in the gardens at the Palace of Versailles. Created by Le Notre, a master of perspective and ordered perfection, the gardens of Versailles embody the rigid architectural theories employed by French garden designers at the time.

Formal French gardens made expert use of linear perspective and proportion. The garden was a basic rectangle divided into a regular grid pattern by alleys and walks all arranged around a central axis. Parterres of clipped box hedges contrasting with gravel were located adjacent to the main building and bordered by walls of high hedges. Along the main axis, avenues of double, and sometimes triple, rows of trees led to a vast forest or a "wilderness," which in reality was not at all wild but a very ordered place of tall hedges and pathways.

This extremely formal style was inspired by concepts developed during the Italian Renaissance. The French built on the Renaissance idea that architecture and garden should be linked, and then further exploited the use of linear perspective with their avenues of trees, alleys and rows of high clipped hedges. Today they are still at the forefront in methods of pruning and shaping. The French also introduced a whole new gardening vocabulary during this period, with garden partitions (parterres), wall-like constructions of trained plants (palisades), vaulted arbors of intertwined branches (berceaux), and forests dissected by walks (bosquets).

The features of the formal French style are still popular and relevant, and can be seen in gardens throughout the

world: clipped parterres and hedges can work beautifully in confined city spaces. Once established, a formal French-style garden is comparatively low maintenance and provides year-round interest with the interplay of textures and shades of greens and grays.

BELOW: Flower-filled boxed parterres are accentuated by pyramid-shaped topiaries. Behind them, the clipped perfection of the high hedge walls provide a lush backdrop.

OPPOSITE: This masterpiece in green shows the skill of the formal French style. A lush carpet of lawn is lined by living walls in varying shades of green. Stone benches, their backs formed from clipped hedge, offer a resting place while two massive columns of clipped beech stand like sentinels at the entrance to the villa.

TOP: Iceberg roses grow in profusion within a neat border of low hedging in this green and white themed cottage garden.

ABOVE: In this traditional cottage garden a gravel pathway is edged with foxgloves, marigolds, *Sisyrinchium*, phlox and roses – 'New Dawn' and 'Perpetue'.

OPPOSITE: A harmonious balance of tones and textures creates a tranquil effect in this cottage garden. The meandering line of purple and red foxgloves, *Campanula* and roses lead the eye through the garden into the distance and bring unity to the color scheme.

# NATURAL STYLES

## Cottage gardens

Cottage gardens are intrinsically about profusion, abundance and variety. Early cottage gardens were attached to workers' cottages and the household grew all of its requirements in the one plot. Medicinal herbs, vegetables, fruit trees and flowers were all crammed together in a haphazard manner, most likely together with pigs, chickens and rabbits. Apart from the livestock, not much has changed. Today's cottage gardens are still characterized by an abundance of many different flowers and are typically enclosed by stone walls, picket fences or hedges.

Essentially, cottage garden plants are those that have been grown in this way for hundreds of years. Sometimes called "old-fashioned," cottage plants commonly include lavenders, primroses, white lilies, pinks, honeysuckles, hollyhocks, hawthorns, amaranthus, daisies, daffodils, columbines, geraniums, campanulas and foxgloves. But in fact many types of plants are grown in cottage gardens around the world—the only requirements are that the plant suits the theme and thrives in the location. Roses, on the other hand, are nearly always to be found in the cottage garden, gracing garden beds, framing doorways, sprawling across trellises, and climbing walls.

At Giverny in Normandy, French artist Claude Monet created an extensive cottage garden with winding pathways bordered by flowerbeds bursting with daisies, asters, nasturtiums, geraniums and sunflowers. Wire archways and trellises support climbing roses, clematis, morning glory and jasmine, and wooden bridges arch ponds filled with waterlilies. The result is the exuberant and lush sanctuary where Monet produced many of his best paintings.

Cottage gardens today are just as appealing as they were hundreds of years ago. Apart from the old-world charm these gardens present, the style is attractive to the modern gardener for many reasons. The profusion and abundance of plants is stimulating, especially to the creative gardener, and also provides a sense of enclosure and privacy. In addition, the dense planting style discourages weed growth and requires very little maintenance.

## The influence of the Arts and Crafts Movement

When cottage industries were at their peak in the early nineteenth century, craftsmen and artisans took up cottage gardening, some even specializing in producing certain types of flowers. However, while the "real" cottage gardening continued amongst the working classes throughout the Victorian era, gardens of the upper classes took on a contrived look.

The latter part of the nineteenth century was a period of experimentation and avid plant collection, with both botanists and amateur collectors traveling the world to find new specimens and developing exciting hybrids. As a result, gardens became more about displaying eclectic plant collections than about style or design, and plants were carefully arranged, as if in an art gallery.

Then in the early twentieth century the Arts and Crafts Movement emerged, largely as a reaction to the industrialization of the Victorian era. It pushed for the return of a more natural style of garden. The English garden writer William Robinson railed against the stiff formality of Victorian gardens and advocated natural gardens full of hardy plants, preferably natives. Robinson preached that plants should be located next to others with the same requirements, so that natural drifts would develop. His influence on garden style was widespread and long lasting—the term "Robinsonian" sprang up to describe gardens based on his principles.

ABOVE: A perennial border of dahlias, sunflowers, *Berberis*, fennel, *Kniphofia*, *Crocomisia* and *Heuchera* create a rich display in this English-style garden.

LEFT: There is a sense of abundance in this English style garden with its series of densely planted garden beds and massed plantings of *Delphinium*, *Stachys* and *Allium*, all contained within neatly clipped box hedges.

## The "English" garden and perennial borders

Gertrude Jekyll is credited with creating what became known as the "English" garden style, characterized by a skilful combination of formal structure with a seemingly informal combination of plants, particularly perennial borders. Originally trained in art, Jekyll used plants in much the same way as an artist uses paints, creating complex combinations of trees, shrubs, perennials, biennials, annuals, bulbs and potted plants, all arranged to support particular color schemes.

Drawing on William Robinson's principles of natural style, Jekyll created elaborate borders and flowerbeds in gardens she designed for clients both in England and the United States. However, her true genius lay in her ability to create the appearance of informality and abandon within a rigid architectural structure. She collaborated with architects of the time, in particular Edwin Lutyens, helping to bridge the gap between their more rigid architectural approach to gardens and the concepts of the naturalistic movement. Her widespread influence can still be seen in perennial borders in modern gardens around the world.

BELOW: A gravel path cuts through a perennial border of mass plantings of *Phlomis*, *Senecio*, *Cotinus*, *Berberis*, *Allium* and *Alchemilla mollis*.

OPPOSITE: The sophisticated planting schemes in Gertrude Jekyll's perennial borders had a lasting influence on garden style throughout the western world as can be seen in these borders, all based on Jekyll's schemes. Combining formal structure with seemingly informal plant combinations, Jekyll created borders that cleverly combined balance and repetition of color, texture and plant shape. 'Hot' flower tones of orange, reds and scarlet were used with cooler yellows and blues in complementary contrast.

## The landscape movement

One of the first influential garden designers to break away from the rigid structure of the formal styles was Lancelot "Capability" Brown, whose grand, sweeping gardens were based on the beauty of the natural English landscape. In the eighteenth century Brown removed many existing French-style formal gardens, and in their place created parkland-style gardens featuring lakes, rivers and woodlands and encircled with belts of trees.

The essence of the natural gardening movement was to allow plants rather than architecture to dictate the form of the garden. In practice though, the "natural" philosophy was often combined with a more structured style, and many designers and gardeners used the Renaissance principle of having geometric formal layouts close to the house and a less structured, natural style further away from it.

In the early 1900s the Italians continued to influence garden styles, but the naturalistic ethos was also evident. Later, designers such as Beatrix Farrand and Charles Platt in the United States and Harold Peto in England and the south of France combined formal features such as topiary, hedging and geometric layouts with informal planting and naturalized drifts of perennials. In Australia the natural style was made popular by Edna Walling, whose gardens featured winding pathways, massed drifts of plants and stone walls built by local craftsmen.

In England the American amateur gardener Lawrence Johnston developed a new style of gardening that has had a lasting influence on gardens throughout the world. At Hidcote in Gloucestershire, now owned by the English National Trust, Johnston created a series of garden compartments or rooms, each with its own planting theme or color scheme. Within these formal settings of high clipped hedges, he used very informal plantings inspired by the teachings of Gertrude Jekyll. It is this combination of rigid formality and wild abandon that continues to attract and inspire gardeners and designers across different cultures. It is a style that transfers well to urban gardens where space constraints mean that structure and order is important but at the same time it allows plenty of scope for personal expression and creativity.

ABOVE LEFT: Curved garden beds and sweeping lawns and trees underplanted with drifts of smaller perennials create a less structured, "natural" style.

ABOVE RIGHT: More formal, geometric garden beds planted close to the house can effectively link architecture and garden.

OPPOSITE: Gardens continue to combine formal settings with informal plantings, a style that developed in the early 20th century. In these gardens drifts of perennials have been allowed to naturalize, sometimes in combination with formal features such as clipped borders and topiary shapes.

## THE NATURALIZED GARDEN

While the seeds had been sown by Capability Brown in the 1700s, the true "naturalistic" garden style, with its curved garden bends winding under canopies of trees, only came into its own in the 1930s, when Architect Frank Lloyd Wright, with his innovative ideas on the relationship between buildings and landscape, starting working in the American Midwest with Danish immigrant and garden designer Jens Jensen.

Jensen's designs were characterized by broad open meadows bordered by woodland and tree-lined trails. They also included more formal, geometric garden beds close to the house, which featured "cutting beds" full of old-fashioned flowers. His gardens were carefully planned so that plants were used to maximum effect with sunlight, shadow and color. For example, plants with silver and gray foliage were planted where they would be illuminated by rising sun and mist, and trees with dramatic red autumn leaves where they would be highlighted by the setting sun. Another characteristic planting scheme of Jensen's was flowering dogwood and hawthorn trees underplanted with wildflowers.

THIS PAGE: The dramatic silver foliage of this *Elaeagnus* 'Quicksilver' is enhanced in this garden by placing it where it will be lit up by the early morning light.

OPPOSITE: Drifts of brilliant yellow *Achillea filipendulina* 'Gold Plate' and *Rudbeckia* (top left), bluebells (top right and bottom left) and daffodils (bottom right) have been allowed to naturalize in these woodland settings, creating a wonderful carpet of color.

Contemporary naturalist designers such as Wolfgang Oehme and James van Sweden, who pioneered the "New American" style, have perfected the art of designing a garden to appear as if it were not designed at all. Like Gertrude Jekyll's complex combinations, the unstructured, natural appearance of Oehme and van Sweden's sweeping borders of perennials and grasses belies the careful planning behind them. These finely executed combinations of texture, color and abstract patterns are planned down to the finest detail to provide year-round interest.

The naturalistic garden style is perfect for small rectangular garden plots because the curved garden beds and freeform island beds and mounds help to disguise the straight perimeters. Grasses can be chosen for their strong vertical lines and architectural features, or for the opposite effect, with soft, wispy varieties helping to mute boundaries and make a small space appear larger. Using native or local plants also reduces the need for pesticides and water, and attracts birds and insects to the garden.

TOP: This grass garden creates a rich interplay of colors and textures. From back left: *Miscanthus*, *Panicum virgatum* 'Rotstrahlbusch', *Festuca glauca*, *Pennisetum* 'Woodside' and *Sedum*.

MIDDLE: Ornamental grasses billow down a terraced path, blurring the boundaries and softening lines.

BOTTOM: The deep purple tones and attractive flower heads of the edible herb *Perilla* makes a dramatic contrast to the delicate pronged foliage of *Miscanthus sinensis* 'Gracillimus' and the spiky *Carex*.

OPPOSITE: Ornamental grasses can be combined with perennials to stunning effect. Here the golden glow of *Calamagrostis* provides a brilliant background for white Echinacea flowers, yellow *Rudbeckia* and bright crimson *Helenium*.

## ORIENTAL INSPIRATION

Oriental gardens such as those found in China and Japan draw their inspiration from the beauty of the natural landscape, relying on simplicity of form and flowing lines to create balance and harmony. Materials are carefully chosen to complement each other and to represent elements of the natural landscape. Perfect for small spaces, and with the emphasis on creating a peaceful haven from the outside world, it is a styles that particularly appeals to modern urban dwellers.

The influence of oriental styles began to appear in gardens of the West in the eighteenth century, when travelers to Japan and China returned inspired by a new approach to landscape design. The Japanese style, where each detail symbolized an element of the natural landscape, offered an exotic contrast to the rigid formality of eighteenth-century European gardens. The Japanese influence widened during the nineteenth century, when plant collectors brought back exotic species of maples, azaleas, bamboos, camellias and magnolias.

This interest in new ideas and plants coincided with the natural garden movement led in England by William Robinson. New Asiatic species were popular in the "natural-style" gardens that were springing up in both America and England, where rhododendrons, dogwoods, roses, maples and magnolias were underplanted with drifts of Japanese irises, blue poppies, primulas and gentians. In New York, the prominent nineteenth-century landscape architect Frederick Law Olmsted converted 800 acres of rocky land in Manhattan into a naturalized landscape of lakes, woodlands and pavilions to create Central Park.

MAIN IMAGE: The red of the pavilion in this traditional Japanese garden contrasts with, yet complements, the tranquility of the scene. This constant interplay of contrasting yet complementary elements is fundamental to both Chinese and Japanese garden design.

INSET TOP: The Himalayan poppy (*Meconopsis*) was one of the many plants introduced to Western gardens during the 18th century, when travelers returned from Japan and China inspired by the designs and exotic plants of the orient.

INSET BOTTOM: Stands of bamboo are appealing on several levels – they add a vertical element, they provide effective screening and their delicate foliage is not only visually pleasing, it adds the element of sound with its soft rustling whenever there is a breeze.

The Japanese influence can also be seen in well-known gardens such as Claude Monet's at Giverny, in Normandy. Monet, along with other Impressionists of the time, was particularly interested in Japanese art and collected Japanese woodcuts. His admiration for Japanese gardens and aesthetics inspired the design for his lily pond and its famous arched bridge, the only variation being that the bridge was painted blue–green rather than the traditional vermilion used in Japanese gardens.

"Designed landscapes" such as those of English garden designer Russell Page make strong use of many of the oriental garden techniques and reveal something of the essence of the Japanese and Chinese aesthetic. Developed in response to the site and deferring to nature, Page's gardens feature trees and shrubs planted in groups around open lawns, ponds and streams and tranquil woodlands. Open stretches of lawn direct the eye to pathways that wind out of sight, creating anticipation and inviting exploration. Pathways pass through a series of landscape scenes, but unlike those in formal gardens, these "rooms" emulate the natural landscape, with sweeping curves rather than geometric lines.

In Chinese and Japanese gardens, balance is sought through the interplay of complementary but contrasting elements—yin and yang, rough and smooth, vertical and horizontal, light and shade, water and rock, mountain and plain. Symmetry is avoided and elements such as stones are

arranged in groups of three, five and seven. Some of the significance of stones in the oriental garden comes from Buddhist traditions. In Buddhist gardens nine stones, five upright and four lying flat, represent the nine spirits of the Buddhist pantheon. Beyond this symbolism, stones are placed so that their position appears natural and harmonious with other elements, such as water and plants.

Two characteristic styles of Japanese garden design are the tea garden and the abstract garden. The tea garden developed around the ritualized tea ceremony, which encourages characteristics such as humility, restraint and sensibility. Guests approach the tea house through a highly stylized garden that aims to create the spiritual atmosphere associated with particular landscapes, such as the lonely austerity of an alpine terrain or the mystery of secluded woodlands.

The abstract garden uses natural materials such as gravel, stones and water, rather than plants, to represent the elements of nature. These are placed in artful arrangements—for example a large single rock rising above a sea of raked gravel—which give the abstract garden an effect almost like a three-dimensional painting.

Sound and scent are also accentuated in the traditional Japanese garden. Fragrant climbers such as wisteria and clematis and flowering fruit trees fill the garden with scent in spring, the falling blossoms creating a delicate carpet. Autumn color is provided by the brilliant tones of maples and other deciduous shrubs and trees. The rustling of bamboo and the sound of water running over stones add to the serenity.

The design principles used in oriental gardens can be used effectively in a contemporary courtyard garden. Elegant simplicity and attention to detail work well in a confined space. Change and variation can be achieved through contrasts in texture and form, movement suggested by winding pathways and rippling water, and mystery evoked through the careful placement of screens and hidden views.

In oriental gardens, plants are chosen for the beauty of their shape and form, and this is often emphasized through clipping and training or placement with contrasting materials. Trees and hedges are clipped into distinctive shapes or to emulate the form of rocks, the lushness of green moss is accentuated by shaping it into mounds within a bed of white gravel, and stands of delicate bamboo add a strong vertical element as well as provide screening.

PAGE 40, CLOCKWISE FROM TOP LEFT: A stone water feature nestles amongst a bamboo stand; lily ponds have provided inspiration for many an artist, including Claude Monet, who created his own in his garden at Giverny. In this one a stone cherub contemplates the view; like yin and yang, these rocks and moss bring opposite and complementary elements together; in Japanese abstract gardens the elements of a landscape are represented in a highly stylized fashion. Here, in this gravel garden, a river landscape is created in miniature, with pebbles used to represent the tumbling water of a stream.

PAGE 41: A tranquil view from a Japanese garden pavilion inspires contemplation, white stepping stones winding out of sight, inviting the viewer to discover what is beyond.

ABOVE: The Japanese *Clematis Haku Ookan* has wonderfully showy flowers, the white stamens making a stark contrast against the deep purple of the petals.

OPPOSITE, CLOCKWISE FROM TOP LEFT: The gray tones of the curved wooden bridge are so perfectly matched with the scene that it appears to float above the lily pond; Japanese cherry blossoms make a delicate carpet of pink as they fall; the beauty of these stones is enhanced by the constant play of water across their surface; the Japanese maple, *Acer palmatum*, is prized for its brilliant deep red foliage

# Defining the
# Boundaries

# DEFINING THE BOUNDARIES

The notion of enclosure has been fundamental to garden design through the ages. From the classical gardens of ancient Rome to contemporary courtyards of the twenty-first century, the garden has functioned as a haven from the outside world.

How you define the boundaries of your garden will determine a great deal about its character. The type of structures and materials chosen for walls, fences and gates will help set the mood of the garden and define the way it will be used. Solid walls create a sense of complete enclosure, while open fences allow views of the world beyond the garden's boundaries. Stone, whether natural or reconstructed, concrete, timber, metal, willow and bamboo are just some of the possible materials.

Apart from their role in defining the outer periphery of the garden, walls, fences and screens also shape internal spaces. These boundary structures must be carefully planned: they are costly to construct, and will affect many later decisions, such as planting designs and flooring.

BELOW LEFT: Natural stone walls have a warmth and charm that is hard to beat. In this garden, the stone retaining wall sets the mood for a peaceful sitting area.

BELOW RIGHT: A red painted wall decorated with brightly colored ceramic fish is a strong focal point.

OPPOSITE: An electric blue wall in this cosy nook provides a vibrant background for the decorative mosaic wall plaque.

## LEVELS AND RETAINING WALLS

Planning the levels in the garden is one of the first and most important tasks that you will face, and too often it is overlooked. A change of level adds interest and can create a sense of space, particularly in small gardens. It can allow you to bring an element of surprise into your garden by keeping sections partly or completely hidden from view, revealing them gradually as you move through the garden. Even in very small gardens this is possible by changing levels.

Where the garden is situated on a slope, two or more levels can be created, and even where the garden is essentially flat, a change of levels can be introduced. If the level is to be changed significantly, or you plan to change the ground surface, say from grass to paving, it is important to consider the drainage implications. It is worth seeking professional advice if you are uncertain about drainage requirements, as poor drainage can be difficult and expensive to remedy.

A change of levels will usually involve the construction of retaining walls. When choosing materials for constructing retaining walls, use the architectural style of the house as a guiding factor. Using the same or similar materials in your garden instantly links the two, bringing unity and making the garden feel like an extension of the inside living space. In most instances, though, it is the change of levels, not the retaining wall, that is being featured, and the retaining wall becomes a backdrop for your planting scheme. Planting in front of, on or above a wall can soften hard surfaces and effectively blur the divisions between different sections of the garden.

Construction of retaining walls may be regulated by local authorities, so it is important to check for any building specifications before you begin construction. Materials, construction methods, drainage, reinforcement and foundation depth must all be considered. The depth of the foundations will depend on factors such as the size and weight of the wall and the pressure exerted by the soil behind it. Drainage is essential, and should be carefully planned. A drain at the base, along the length of the retaining wall, as well as drainage holes at regular intervals within the wall, will allow excess water to drain away, removing the risk of the wall collapsing. Pebbles or small boulders encased in wire meshing make attractive retaining walls and have the added advantage of not needing concrete footings or drains because of their open structure.

TOP: The change of levels in this dramatic but simple courtyard create a sense of space and invite visitors to move towards the sitting area. The sense of movement is accentuated through the color scheme, the red of the steps echoed in the focal point on the rear wall.

ABOVE: Natural stone retaining walls on this steeply terraced garden are softened by cascading foliage.

OPPOSITE, TOP: A small change of level adds interest to this garden, the stone steps and brick pillars drawing the eye and encouraging further exploration of the garden.

OPPOSITE BOTTOM: Brightly colored terraces double as a feature and area for seating.

## WALLS

Walls are the quintessential elements of enclosure. Walled gardens carry an aura of seclusion, serenity and abundance. They bring to mind the romance of the enclosed Medieval garden, *hortus conclusus*, which was built for the purpose of entertaining and repose and filled with sweetly scented flowers and herbs.

Walls are also one of the gardener's greatest allies, and can help solve many horticultural and design challenges—they provide privacy, hide unattractive areas such as tool sheds or utility areas, can be used to create a sense of distance, and can act as a palette for artistic expression. Of course, walls also provide a permanent support structure for climbing or espaliered plants.

OPPOSITE: Bold but simple, the smoothness and deep ochre color of this molded concrete seat is dramatically set off by the deep blue of the wall.

BELOW: Corrugated iron used in the boundary wall adds texture to this small garden and highlights the silver color theme in the garden beds. The beautifully detailed timber retaining walls also double as seating.

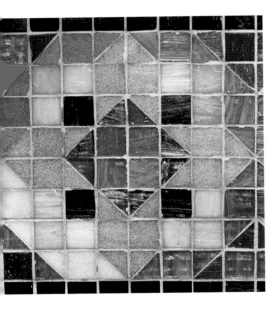

There is an enormous range of materials available for building walls. Stone is one of the most attractive materials—it is strong, weathers beautifully and is the perfect host for mosses and lichen. A stone wall is a considerable investment, but it is a lasting feature that will enhance your garden in many ways. Brick is another attractive long-lasting alternative with many choices of color and texture. A brick wall can be a feature in itself, or it can be used as a foil for plants, or painted, rendered or bagged.

Walls can be painted to create many different effects in the garden. For example, a dark green wall will blend into the background, giving the illusion of more space, while a white-painted wall can provide a delightful backdrop for flowering plants or classically clipped hedges and archways. In the Latin-style garden, a feature wall of vibrant blue can be used to echo the blue of the sky, visually extending the garden outward and upward. A large wall at the rear of the garden may be the perfect canvas for a dramatic trompe l'oeil.

Modern techniques for constructing walls include using stone, such as limestone, granite or sandstone, as cladding over concrete blocks. This is a useful method for linking garden walls with paving or with the materials used in the house; and while not exactly inexpensive, it does give you the effect of stone at a lower cost than if you were to use solid stone for the entire wall.

Rendering is a great way to cover unattractive concrete blocks or old brickwork without blowing your budget. Rendered walls provide a smooth finish that can be left unadorned (for a natural sandy-colored look) or painted (to create a feature wall). Mosaic or patterned tiling is another way to beautifully finish rendered walls, and can turn a previously dull corner of the garden into a favorite nook.

TOP: Climbing plants are trained along a dark blue wall in this lush corner.

MIDDLE: A rendered wall can be the perfect spot for colorful mosaics.

BOTTOM: The bright pink and yellow of cascading *Aubrieta* and *Aurinia saxatilis* makes a colorful display on a stone retaining wall.

OPPOSITE, TOP: A high wall is partly rendered and partly natural brick to create an interesting contrast in texture and color. A series of low, black walls make interesting features and also double as benches.

OPPOSITE, LEFT: The warm yellow of this high rendered wall complements the blue and yellow water feature and wall tiles.

OPPOSITE, MIDDLE: An elaborate mosaic wall mural makes a vibrant feature of these curved walls.

OPPOSITE, RIGHT: The rustic charm of this roughly rendered wall is highlighted by the detail in the elaborate carved timber inset.

## FENCES AND GATES

Your choice of garden fence is a design statement in itself, and reveals much about the style of the garden within. The architecture of the house is a strong guiding factor here, as is the style of the garden. A timber picket fence is often associated with the informality of a cottage-style garden, while a tall wrought-iron fence and grand entrance would complement a more formal or minimalist garden style. A high brick wall will give privacy and block out traffic noise on a busy street; where there is a view beyond the garden, a sculptural fence of wire could do the trick.

Timber fences are both practical and attractive, and offer a number of construction options. One of the most basic forms of timber fence uses a series of upright support posts and two horizontal rails to which vertical planks are attached. The vertical planks can be spaced to create a more open fence or, for maximum privacy, they can be overlapped. The lengths of the planks can be varied, or the tops shaped, for a distinctive, decorative look. Timber fences are easily painted: To make them a feature, use a bright color or a color that highlights and matches the house. For a less visible boundary, a more natural color such as blue–gray, brown or green will blend with the surrounding environment.

There are two types of timber used for building. Hardwood (such as cedar) is more expensive, but will last ten to twenty years with the right treatment. If you choose the cheaper option of softwood (such as pine), maintenance will be more of an issue, as you will need to regularly paint or stain the fence to preserve it.

Picket fences, with their pointed tops, have a charm all of their own, and are usually associated with cottage gardens. They allow glimpses of the garden and look wonderful with a profusion of flowers peeping through the gaps. If you want to create more character, use pickets with rounded or square-cut ends or paint the fence a bright color.

TOP RIGHT: A blue picket fence defines the boundary and has a warm, welcoming effect.

RIGHT: This high trellis fence creates privacy and is an attractive feature in this tropical courtyard.

OPPOSITE, CLOCKWISE FROM TOP LEFT: This rustic timber fence works beautifully against a profusion of cottage garden flowers; a painted trellis fence adds a strong vertical element and acts as a support for clematis; the feathery foliage of cotinus cascades over a criss-cross fence; colorful anemones and white tulips stand out in stark relief against a white timber fence.

Metal is a versatile material in the garden. For fences, screens and gates it offers many options in style, weight and price. Traditional wrought iron is perfect for formal gardens and classical architecture, and modern metal products can be used in so many ways. Some of these new products are also light in weight or available pre-cut, making construction easy. Corrugated iron, aluminum sheets, metal mesh panels and galvanized steel are all ideal for garden structures. Steel rods, usually used to reinforce concrete, can be arranged in interesting patterns to create internal divisions in the garden; or use copper piping, which has the added advantage of weathering to the lovely tones of verdigris.

Gates need to be practical, but they can be beautiful too, and enhance the character of the garden. It is important to choose a gate that fits the purpose and suits the garden design. For example, an eye-catching, welcoming gate might be the ideal entrance to your garden, but a solid gate is more suitable if privacy or security is a major issue. Sometimes a plain and simple gate is the most appropriate, or the gate could be a decorative feature that echoes some other aspect of the garden.

The vast array of materials which can be used for gates ensures that you can choose a design to suit any style of garden. You could opt for natural-looking materials such as timber—whether solid, carved, trellis or picket—or woven willow or bamboo. Metal offers a great range of choices for both modern and traditional gates, including tubular steel or iron, painted, galvanized or powder-coated. It can also be used to create tailor-made gates, and allows great scope for artisans to achieve unusual and stunning effects using beaten copper or bronze or a combination of materials.

LEFT: An ornate metal gate enhances the entrance to a formal garden.

OPPOSITE, CLOCKWISE FROM TOP LEFT: This custom-made metal fence with resin sea sculptures links the garden with the view of the sea beyond; the arched timber gate is echoed in the sculpted hedge; a spiral metal gate makes a distinctive feature; timber posts with wire arch frames the view in a country garden.

## SCREENS

Screens provide an element of mystery and discovery in the garden. They make the garden infinitely more pleasing because it is not visible in its entirety from any one spot. Screens can also be used to create "rooms" within the garden, as well as to hide the utility areas, such as compost heaps, you don't want to be seen. Even in small gardens, screens can be used effectively to define spaces; this will also help make the garden appear larger.

The choice of materials which may be used for screening is infinite. Screens can be made with trees, shrubs, hedges or climbing plants on a trellis or similar support structure; or, more creatively, with topiary shapes or by training plants into horizontal growing patterns through espalier or pleaching (see pages 123–127). Beautiful screens may be created using bamboo or woven willow or hazel, or you could opt for highly ornate wrought iron or Moorish fretwork. Most fencing materials of timber or metal can be used to make excellent screens, whether solid or open, and are long-lasting alternatives.

For a contemporary look, screens made of translucent materials such as solid glass, stiffened plastic mesh, plastic sheeting, muslin or glass blocks can be used as stunning features. Glass blocks or bricks are particularly versatile, as they can be placed within a solid wall constructed of rendered cement blocks or brick. Other modern combinations include sections of contrasting materials on a screen or wall; for example, dry stone walls with smooth rendered sections, or polished metal with sections of wood. Plastic piping can be used to make innovative screens that act as support structures for trailing and climbing plants, and some pipes may also be used as planting containers.

BELOW: Patterned perspex screens instantly imbue this garden with a Moroccan flavor.

OPPOSITE, CLOCKWISE FROM TOP LEFT: A yellow fabric screen provides a vibrant backdrop for a purple clematis; garden rooms or compartments can be created with tall hedges, the arches allowing a glimpse of what is beyond; a latticework screen supports a grapevine and is the perfect host for colorful lichen; a woven screen with mirror insert visually expands a small tropical courtyard.

## HEDGES

Hedges were traditionally an invaluable element of the garden. They were used as fences, screens and windbreaks, to define boundaries and provide privacy, but also as an architectural device to link buildings with the garden, create order and formality, or simply unify a garden design.

The art of designing with hedges was executed with great skill during the Renaissance, when hedges became the main architectural elements of the garden. Hedges were used to create rooms, corridors and other garden spaces; they provided structure, framed vistas, directed the eye, and acted as screens to obscure parts of the garden from view.

In the formal French gardens of the sixteenth and seventeenth centuries, hedge clipping was taken to great heights. Not only were hedges integral to the design and mood of the formal French garden; they were also key ornamentations, clipped to perfection into elaborate patterns. In Elizabethan knot gardens, hedges gave definition and sophistication to otherwise simple plantings of lavender, rosemary and common cottage plants.

RIGHT, FROM TOP DOWN: A tightly clipped hedge gives definition to a lavender-filled garden bed; a copper beech hedge makes a decorative living fence, the orange gate enhances the copper tones throughout the garden; old-fashioned roses such as *Rosa* 'Madame Alfred Carriere' and *Rosa* 'Aloha' can be trained to form a beautiful screening hedge; two different conifer varieties, *Thuja occidentalis* and *Chamaecyparis lawsoniana* cvs, have been artfully trained to form a multicolored hedge.

OPPOSITE, CLOCKWISE FROM TOP LEFT: There is a pleasing juxtaposition of textures, tone and line in this combination of a tightly clipped conifer hedge underlining a row of *Prunus* 'Kanzan'.

Where there is enough space, hedges can be used to separate areas of the garden or provide a transition, such as from formal to informal areas. A whole new element is introduced when a window or archway is cut into the hedge, as this can allow a view into another garden area or frame a vista or a feature such as a fountain or sculpture. Gaps in hedges can also be placed to allow light into an area of the garden.

Formal hedges can be used to define hard-surfaced areas such as paved courtyards and driveways, and when planted along the edges of pathways they emphasize their direction and form. Hedges will also accentuate entrances: a low hedge will lead the eye to the entrance, while a high hedge will give a sense of something contained beyond. Contrasting hedges with other plant textures and colors will add visual depth, and can make a dramatic statement, such as when a hedge of dark green box is paired with a border of silvery gray foliage such as lamb's ears.

For a softer effect, use plants which will grow naturally into informal hedges, such as evergreen shrubs and perennials with dense foliage. Camellias, with their glossy leaves, are attractive year-round but make an impressive display in flower, as do rambling or climbing roses grown as an informal hedge or screen. Santolina or lavender, while suitable for clipped low hedges, can also be lightly shaped to create a less formal border. Grasses and spiky tuft-forming plants such as mondo grass and autumn crocus also work well as informal low borders.

# HEDGE AND SCREENING PLANTS

*Buxus sempervirens* (Box)—This small-leaved evergreen shrub is a favorite for formal hedges. Also used as low edging, in knot gardens and for topiary. It is fairly slow growing and prefers sun or part shade.

*Camellia sasanqua* (Camellia)—This fast-growing tall evergreen shrub has beautiful dark green glossy leaves and single flowers in pink or white. It can be grown as a hedge or screen, along a fence or wall.

*Carpinus betulus* (Hornbeam)—A deciduous small-leaved tree that responds well to clipping and is great for topiary and hedging. It is reasonably hardy, and likes full sun.

*Fagus sylvatica* (Beech)— This deciduous tree can be used to create a lovely thick hedge. It has light green leaves in spring that turn a brilliant golden in autumn.

*Hebe vernicosa* (Hebe)—This evergreen shrub has a compact shape and dense foliage, with white flowers in spring and summer. It can be clipped to shape and is good in borders.

*Hedera helix* (Ivy)—This versatile climber can be grown on walls, fences, screens and wire structures or topiary shapes. Clipping will keep it under control.

*Ilex* species (Holly)—Most of the evergreen holly species and cultivars can be grown as hardy hedging plants or clipped into topiary shapes.

*Laurus nobilis* (Bay)—Also valued for its culinary uses, this hardy evergreen tree can be clipped into topiary shapes or planted in screens.

*Ligustrum* species (Privet)—This low-growing evergreen shrub has small oval leaves and, like box, is favored for hedges, edging and topiary.

*Mackaya bella* (Mackaya)—An evergreen shrub with dense branches, dark glossy leaves and large mauve or pink flowers. Best in subtropical to temperate climates, where it can be grown as a hedge or screen.

*Murraya paniculata* syn. *exotica* (Orange jessamine)—With its dark green glossy leaves and highly fragrant flowers that look and smell like orange blossom, this evergreen shrub makes a very attractive screen or hedge.

*Taxus baccata* (Yew)—Its dark green dense foliage and hardy evergreen habit make yew perfect for clipping into hedges or topiary. A favorite for centuries.

*Tilia platyphyllos* (Lime)—Also known as the linden, this deciduous tree has a spreading habit and is favored for pleaching as well as for clipping into topiary shapes.

*Viburnum tinus* (Laurustinus)—This evergreen shrub has a compact and dense habit with large leaves and white flowers in late winter and spring. It's ideal for hedging, responding well to clipping and shaping.

BELOW: A border of tightly clipped *Buxus sempervirens* leads the eye to a decorative urn.

OPPOSITE, TOP: Hedges have been formed into topiary shapes throughout this formal garden and as a border along the boundary.

OPPOSITE, BOTTOM LEFT: Hedges are used to great effect in this formal English-style garden, defining the edges of the flower beds and forming a high boundary screen.

OPPOSITE, BOTTOM RIGHT: A pleasing balance is achieved in this large garden, with the sharp horizontal line of dark green hedges acting as a perfect foil to the sweeping lawns and delicate foliage of the silver birches.

At
Ground
Level

# AT GROUND LEVEL

It's not just the plants and vertical structures that define your garden; what happens on the ground is just as important for setting the mood—whether you choose a carpet of living groundcover or lawn, or versatile, long-lasting concrete, or an intricately laid mosaic of pebbles and stone.

The design of your garden at ground level will be governed by its overall style, the architecture of the house, and the purpose of the area. Apart from their practical purposes, pathways and hard-surface areas can be attractive features in themselves, and they also provide a contrasting texture to that of the plants, breaking up the "green" so that the garden remains visually interesting and dynamic. Pathways are rather like the arteries of your garden, directing the traffic flow and bringing it to life in both a practical and aesthetic sense. Areas which are finished with hard surfaces can act as a transition between indoors and outdoors, provide a place for entertaining and dining, and also act as focal points for ornamentation or other features.

TOP: Timber rounds make very attractive stepping stones, particularly in a natural-style garden like this one.

BOTTOM: A zigzag path of stone set into a soft mossy groundcover is further accentuated by a border of ivy.

OPPOSITE: Stone pathways have a wonderful warmth and texture that invites exploration. Here, the pathway highlights the abundance of the flowerbeds and leads the eye to a rose-covered arbor.

# PATHWAYS AND HARD SURFACES

Pathways are practical, but they also add an essential element of human drama to the garden. A pathway winding through the garden, the final destination hidden, is enticing and creates visual interest. A wide straight pathway leading directly to a feature such as a niche or fountain directs the eye to the focal point and gives the garden a sense of proportion and linear perspective. Paths can also be used to divide the garden into sections, or to link the garden as a whole.

Pathways should be designed to suit the amount of traffic they will carry and the style of the garden. A sturdy brick or paved pathway will define the edge of a grass lawn and is also the perfect foil for a mixed border of brightly colored perennials. If a path is to be a major artery, it should be wide enough to allow two people to walk abreast, and it should have a stable, hard-wearing surface. If a pathway is only required for occasional weeding and planting, then width and surface are less significant. Stepping stones—of timber, pavers, concrete or natural stone—dotted through a garden bed allow access and also add texture and visual movement.

BELOW LEFT: A timber walkway allows visitors to walk easily through this grass garden and protects the vegetation from trampling. Its soft weathered appearance is also in keeping with the natural style of the garden.

BELOW RIGHT: Stone set into gravel makes an inviting path alongside a bed of lavender.

High-traffic areas in the garden are best covered with a hard surface for both practical and design reasons. Lawn or groundcovers will not usually survive the wear of high traffic and will have to be continually replaced, while hard surfaces are stable and long lasting. Materials chosen for hard surfaces should complement those used in your house—both the external building and the internal flooring—particularly when the outdoor area is next to the house. Timber decking, for example, will suit an outdoor terrace adjacent to a house with internal timber floors. Equally, if the internal floors are reconstituted stone, using a similar material for outside paving will result in a seamless indoor–outdoor flow.

Hard-surface entertaining areas should be located where they are easily accessible from the house. This might be adjacent to the house or, if slightly removed, easily reached from the house via a pathway or steps. When planning the layout, think about how you envisage using your garden and work out where the most convenient and pleasant area for entertaining would be. But remember that even the most idyllic of outdoor entertaining areas is unlikely to be used much if it is located in the back corner of the garden and can only be reached via several flights of steps.

BELOW: A decorative border and feature of inlaid pebbles visually widens this narrow courtyard and provides relief from the uniformity of tone in the terracotta pavers and rendered walls.

## BRICKS

Bricks are a very durable and attractive option for paved areas and paths. Paving bricks are harder wearing than ordinary house bricks and are available in a wide variety of textures and colors. They work particularly well when the house is also constructed of brick, but make sure to match your brick types—blond brick pavers will not go too well with a red brick house.

Bricks look particularly effective when laid in strong directional patterns such as herringbone or basketweave. To do this, lay the bricks on their sides onto a sand base (or for a firmer base, sand mixed with concrete). They will look best if you use a contrasting edge. For a more contemporary look, use bricks to edge an area paved with limestone or reconstituted stone.

Directional patterns can also be used to visually alter the shape and size of a garden. A herringbone or diamond shape can make your paved area seem larger than it actually is, and a border will give the appearance of a longer space by leading the eye. These are useful tricks for small gardens or for those with a difficult shape, such as very long and narrow or wide and shallow.

TOP: A simple brick edging gives definition to this garden bed and provides textural contrast to the lawn and gravel.

BOTTOM: The pink tones in the bricks add warmth to this pathway and link it visually with the pink of the roses.

OPPOSITE: A circular pattern of brick paving accentuates the central tree and creates a sense of movement.

## PAVING TILES AND PAVERS

Paving tiles are thinner than bricks and come in a wide range of colors, styles and patterns. Pavers are also available in wedge shapes and small squares, very useful for creating a decorative circular edging around a feature plant or tree.

Terracotta is a popular choice for paving patios and courtyards, its muted rosy tones complementary to greenery. Concrete pavers, contrary to what many people think, can look very attractive, as they come in many different shades, including pink, gray and sandy tones. They are also strong, so can be used in areas where there is heavy traffic (including driveways).

Reconstituted stone is a great alternative to natural stone. It is cheaper, easier to lay and much more readily available than natural stone. Its neat, even appearance is also perfect if you want a smooth, streamlined finish.

Floor tiles are also excellent for garden flooring, but make sure they are suitable for external use. They will not be suitable if they are shiny and slippery. Using the same or similar tiles to those used inside the house can blur the transition between indoors and outdoors, effectively extending the living and entertaining areas. Decorative tiles can also be used for borders or as inserts in paved areas to link the indoor décor with the garden.

BELOW: A checkerboard of thyme enlivens this paved area and links to the rich greens of the topiary shapes behind.

OPPOSITE: Stone slabs set in "crazy paving" style work well with the architecture of the house and planting scheme in this Spanish-style garden.

## STONE

Natural cut stone such as York stone, sandstone or limestone looks wonderful as garden flooring and was once the preferred option. It is now extremely expensive and is more likely to be used for smaller terraces and patios or cut into rectangles or smaller squares to use in borders or edging.

Rough-cut granite slabs are also a very stylish option for small spaces, the dark gray working well with either muted or vividly colored planting schemes. White marble, although expensive, can be used for an Islamic-style courtyard and creates a cool, soothing atmosphere. Smaller marble pieces in black or white can be used with gravel or pebbles for decorative effects or set into paving of a contrasting color as feature tiles.

Slate is also a wonderful material to use with other hard or soft surfaces; however, it is slippery when wet so is best interspersed with rougher textures such as pavers, gravel or groundcovers like mondo grass. Slate can be cut into squares, and is also available as chippings which can be used in place of gravel.

TOP: Natural stone, while expensive, is a stylish choice for paving and can be used in small sections for placing outdoor furniture.

BOTTOM: Pebbles set into the paving make an attractive and highly textured border.

## POURED CONCRETE

Concrete is a wonderfully versatile material, and when poured as a slab provides enormous scope for creativity and personalized finishes. The surface can be smoothed and polished for a contemporary look, or you can set other materials into the still-wet surface to create decorative details. The possibilities are endless—try a feature square of glass bricks, or diamonds of river stones or black pebbles set at regular intervals. Metal or timber strips also work well with natural-colored cement.

A popular treatment for concrete slabs for both internal and external flooring is to mix a colored pigment into the top layer when the cement is being poured. Or the finished slab can be painted with a durable paint suitable for external use; the beauty of this treatment is that you can change the appearance of the flooring at a later date.

## TIMBER

Timber decking is the choice of many for entertaining areas close to the house, particularly where there are internal timber floors. It can also be used for edging on garden beds and for pathways, where it blends beautifully with both plants and other materials such as stone, concrete or metal.

However, due to the plundering of tropical forests and diminishing supplies, timber is now much more expensive than in the past. Commercially grown timbers such as pine are the preferred option for decking and pathways, and recycled timbers such as old railway sleepers make ideal retaining walls, although these are also becoming increasingly scarce.

TOP: Timber combines beautifully with this geometric-shaped lawn to create a strong directional movement. Pockets of plants add interest and textural contrast.

BOTTOM: The richness of timber decking is the perfect balance to these vibrant pink seats set into a turf bench and the willow-weave fencing.

## GRAVEL, PEBBLES AND GLASS CHIPPINGS

Loose, hard surfacing materials are now available in a great range of options, from conventional crushed stone and gravel to new materials such as slate, plastic and glass. Modern chippings have provided an even wider choice in texture and color, from bright blue to black, white, gray and translucent. All can be used to great effect. Chippings can be mixed with pavers to give a softer look, or used to edge a brick pathway as a contrast.

Pebbles are also available in a vast array of colors and sizes. Though it is one of the more expensive options, a pebbly path is a great garden feature. Larger pebbles and rocks can also be placed in garden beds, alongside pathways, and in and around water troughs and ponds. Cobblestones, while uncomfortable to walk on in large areas, can be mixed with other materials for decorative effects. Pebbles can also be set into concrete to create patterns and borders on a hard-surface area or pathway.

TOP RIGHT: A cobblestone path adds a richly textured layer to this grass garden, the color of the bricks working in harmony with the tones of the ornamental grasses.

BOTTOM RIGHT: A dynamic mix of tones and textures has been achieved with this combination of smooth stone pavers set into gray pebbles and a circular feature of pebbles with central concrete insert.

OPPOSITE, CLOCKWISE FROM TOP LEFT: A curved path of white pebbles is dissected to dramatic effect by rows of brick pavers; a sculptural 'snake in the grass' curves its way across a white pebble courtyard; glass bottles have been put to effective use as a decorative border on this gravel path; glass has been extensively used in this predominantly white garden – in the cast-glass furniture, as part of the elevated terrace, as inserts in the walls and in a walkway across the pond.

## METAL, GLASS AND RUBBER

Incorporating materials such as metal, glass and rubber into your garden floor can make it more dynamic. These synthetic materials introduce new textures and colors—metal, plastic and glass can also bring reflective qualities—and inspire uniquely creative treatments. For example, a metal grille can be inserted into a concrete slab and filled with pebbles, gravel or glass chippings. Glass bricks can be set into paving, or glass tiles laid on top of colorful or decorative objects such as marbles. Glass lit from underneath is a wonderfully effective way to light up a dark corner.

Rubber matting is another versatile modern material. It is available in rolls and comes in a variety of textures and colors. Strips of rubber matting can be mixed with other paving materials for a variation in surface textures, or it can be used to cover an entire area such as around a pool. Rubber is nonslip, feels good on bare feet, and is also a very safe surface for children to play on.

BELOW: A raised edge of metal gives strong definition to the tufted grass border and provides a textural contrast with the pebble border and gravel pathway.

OPPOSITE: A floor of chipped rubber has been used in front of this dramatic semi-circular feature wall and water feature. A semi-circular step of cut stone accentuates the line of the wall and highlights the sculptural balls of oak. The wall itself is part rendered and part drystone.

## DECORATIVE DETAILS

In all the great gardens throughout time, it is the decorative details which make them memorable. From the latch on your gate to feature tiles or a trompe l'oeil, decorative detailing is an important part of creating your own distinctive garden, and the hard surfaces of the garden provide many opportunities in this respect.

The creators of Islamic and Roman gardens led the way in these decorations with their use of ornate marble and ceramic floor mosaics. In Spain, the Moors covered every available garden surface with elaborate mosaics in vibrant green, blue, red and yellow. The gardens of Pompeii, still visible today, contain beautifully detailed marble mosaics in muted tones of blue, green and brown combined with black and white. Often marking the entrance to a garden or home, these floor mosaics are typically geometric, laid out in sophisticated linear, rectangular and circular patterns.

When planning a decorative detail, consider the overall mood of your garden. For example, a small, well-placed mosaic may be all that is needed to highlight a paved area. On the other hand, in a highly stylized Latin courtyard, a bold border pattern of brightly colored tiles could be perfect. And in a minimal city garden, a few glass tiles in a concrete floor, or metal strips embedded into steps, could be subtle yet striking details.

TOP: This decorative feature has been created by laying tile strips in a bed of gray pebbles. The pattern is reminiscent of weaving and has a strong suggestion of rotating movement.

CENTER: Patterned panels of tile and pebbles set amongst stone surround a decorative urn and brilliant floral display.

BOTTOM: A brightly tiled table is the ideal background for this glazed pot and succulent.

OPPOSITE: A strong New Mexico flavor in this colorful garden is created with the use of tiles, inlaid pebbles and vibrant blue walls.

## STEPS

Beyond the practical purpose of providing access to different areas and levels of the garden, steps bring a dynamic element by helping to create a mood and emphasizing perspective. Steps tap into the human psyche with their suggestion of leading the way to new areas and unexplored places. We associate steps with actions such as making an entrance or climbing a slope to admire a view. They evoke a response and create expectations on a very fundamental level. And every garden can do with a bit of drama added to the mix.

Visual interest is created when steps lead the eye to another level beyond view, adding an element of surprise or mystery. Steps can also emphasize a focal point, leading upwards to an entrance or archway, or down to a hidden sculpture or water feature. Steps bring structure to the garden and can be used to aesthetically link areas. They can also help to create contrast, providing rough, hard textures against the garden's lush green.

BELOW: Broad stone steps lead upwards to a vine-covered pergola and direct the eye to focal point beyond. The steps are further emphasized by the placement of decorative urns on either side.

OPPOSITE: It is hard to beat the beauty of old stone when it comes to steps. The combination of textured stone and a soft carpet of groundcover such as this *Aubrieta* creates a romantic scene.

Even in the smallest garden it is usually possible to create a change in level and use steps to enliven a flat, dull space. If artificially created, the change of level should be situated where there is a logical alteration in mood or usage. One obvious location is where the area immediately near the house gives way to the rest of the garden. This is a natural transition point and steps can be used to accentuate this. Another would be in the middle area of the garden, particularly if it is long and narrow, as a change of level can help widen the space visually. In a small garden, a single broad step between two levels can serve the dual function by also being a bench, particularly if it is made of tactile material such as timber.

Decisions about steps should be made when you are doing the initial ground plan. Where the steps should go, what style they will be, what materials will be used and how many you need, must all be considered. With steps, safety is also of primary concern.

BELOW LEFT: The sharp geometric lines in this contemporary garden are accentuated by the meticulous detailing of the steeply rising steps.

BELOW RIGHT: The semi-circular brick steps are given height and emphasis by the stone pots and rounded shape of the clipped *Buxus*.

Be generous with size—the most common mistake is to make the steps too small. The treads (the horizontal surface) should be 12–18 inches (30–45 cm) wide, and the riser (vertical surface) 4–6 inches (10–15 cm) in height. The incline will depend largely on the slope of the area where the steps are being placed. If the incline is sharp, it is preferable to include a landing halfway rather than have a single steep flight of steps. A landing also creates the opportunity to place a feature such as a sculpture, decorative pot or sundial.

The materials chosen for steps will be greatly influenced by those used for other hard surfaces. Where possible, the steps should match paving materials or be complementary in texture and color; for example, stone with gravel or timber with stone. Steps may be as simple as timber sleepers cut into a grassy slope, or they may be grand curved entrance stairs of cut stone complete with handrail. If you are planning for the steps to be an architectural feature, or if safety is an issue, you should hire a professional to build them, as they need to be precise.

BELOW LEFT: The sharp lines of these brick steps are softened by seaside daisies (*Erigeron karvinskianus*).

BELOW RIGHT: The soft gray of weathered timber works well with gravel on these steps. The strongly horizontal line of the timber also visually widens the steps.

# SOFT SURFACES

## Grass lawns

Grass lawns are the most common and popular form of soft groundcovering in gardens. Grass is visually appealing and is also a wonderful surface to walk, sit and play on. If you decide on a grass lawn for your garden, it need not be boring—there are so many options available. Lawn looks wonderful when combined with other materials, such as stone, timber or gravel. Imaginative patterns and forms can be created by combining contrasting materials. For example, a checkerboard pattern of lawn and stone pavers creates a striking groundcover, as do grass mounds or sculpted grass shapes emerging out of white gravel.

When planning your lawn, you need to think carefully about the intended use of the area and its positioning. There are many varieties of grass available, both in seed and in turf form. Turf has the obvious advantage of providing an instant lawn, but for the best long-term lawn, seed sown onto a carefully prepared soil base is unbeatable. There are varieties suitable for all sorts of conditions, including lawns for shady areas and tough grasses that cope with high traffic (such as in kids' play areas).

Once established, your lawn will need to be fed periodically with a good lawn fertilizer.

TOP: Lawn is a very popular and appealing soft ground cover. Here, its curved lines run right to the edge of the flower beds, visually extending the garden.

CENTER: Lawn can be used to break up hard surfaces such as gravel and brick paving.

BOTTOM: The lushness of this lawn lends an elegant air and gives a sense of space.

OPPOSITE: A checked pattern of lawn and pavers makes a simple but dramatic feature.

## Aromatic lawns and groundcovers

Groundcovers, as the name suggests, are plants that grow just above soil level, so that their foliage, and often flowers, form a carpet across the garden floor. Many plants with low, spreading habits make excellent groundcovers, whether used simply to fill bare spaces of garden such as under trees or as an alternative to grass lawns or hard surfaces.

For the ultimate sensory groundcover, plant an aromatic lawn of scented groundcovering plants such as chamomile or thyme; both these low-growing, spreading perennials are suitable for low- to medium-traffic areas and will give off a wonderful scent when walked upon. The smaller-leafed, compact types are the most suitable—such as the nonflowering chamomile 'Treneague' and the silver-leafed thyme, which has a lemon scent—particularly in small areas and in paving pockets.

BELOW LEFT: Seaside daisies (*Erigeron karvinskianus*) make a hardy groundcover and mix well with grass and pavers.

BELOW RIGHT: Flowering thyme makes a very attractive and fragrant groundcover. Here, it happily grows on a path of gravel and stone.

OPPOSITE: Chamomile is a wonderful alternative to lawn where there is plenty of sunlight and gives off a strong scent when walked on. Easy to grow, it forms a thick mat of feathery foliage with small daisy-like flowers from spring through to autumn.

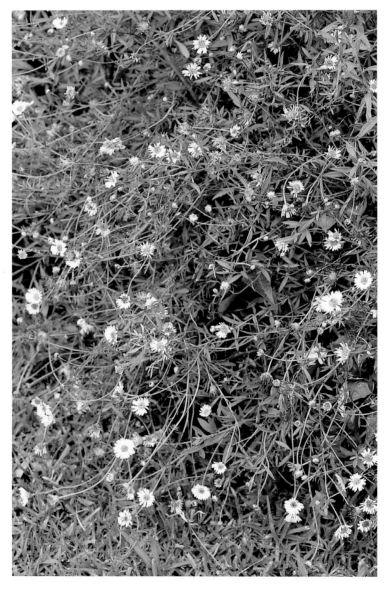

# GROUNDCOVERS

*Ajuga reptans* (Bugle flower)—A mat-forming perennial with rosettes of shiny dark green leaves and long spikes of blue flowers. Some cultivars have variegated or purple-colored foliage. Makes an excellent groundcover, especially in moist soil.

*Alchemilla mollis* (Lady's mantle)—This perennial has pale green rounded leaves with crinkled edges, and tiny yellow flowers in midsummer. Not suitable for traffic areas but ideal as groundcover in garden beds.

*Anthemis nobile* syn. *Chamaemelum nobile* (Chamomile)—An evergreen mat-forming perennial, chamomile has wonderfully aromatic leaves and white daisylike flowers with yellow centers.

*Armeria maritima* (Sea pink)—Hardy evergreen perennials for sandy soil and full sun. They grow in small compact clumps of stiff grasslike leaves, and are well suited to paving edges or pockets. In spring and summer, pink or white flowers appear on tall single stalks.

*Campanula* species (Bellflower)—Many of the perennial bellflowers have low, spreading habits and make ideal groundcovers; for example, the tussock bellflower, *C. carpetica*, which is fast-growing and has pale blue-mauve flowers, and *C. poscharskyana*, which has star-shaped flowers in blue, white or pink.

*Dianthus* species and cultivars (Pinks)—All forms of dianthus make cheerful additions to paved areas or rockeries. They are hardy and like full sun and well-drained soil.

*Erigeron karvinskianus* (Seaside daisy)—A low-growing, spreading perennial with fine leaves and tiny white daisylike flowers. It is low maintenance, and fairly drought tolerant.

*Sedum* species and cultivars (Stonecrop)—This large family of hardy succulents includes many groundcovering plants such as the golden-colored *S. acre* 'Aureum', which forms a dense mat of tiny leaves. Most stonecrops are drought resistant and will grow with very little soil.

*Thymus* species and cultivars (Thyme)—A favorite for scented groundcover, both in aromatic lawns and within paving. *T. praecox* is a compact mat-forming perennial with deep green aromatic leaves and purple flowers in summer.

The silver-leafed thyme, *T. x citriodorus*, has a lemon scent and flavor.

*Tropaeolum majus* (Nasturtium)—This edible fast-growing, trailing groundcover has bright green round leaves and trumpet-shaped flowers in many shades of yellow to red.

*Viola* species (Violets)—There are many species and cultivars of these favored perennials which make ideal groundcovers, especially in shady parts of the garden. The sweet violet, *V. odorata*, is vigorous growing and has famously fragrant flowers.

## PRAIRIES AND MEADOWS

A prairie or meadow planting is a popular way of achieving a more natural-looking garden as well as covering much ground space. Even in a small urban garden it is possible to set aside an area where plants are allowed to naturalize or grow in drifts, beside grassed areas, along paths, underneath trees and on banks.

The prairie style was developed by architect Frank Lloyd Wright and landscape designer Jens Jensen in the American Midwest during the 1930s (see page 35). With its focus on creating entire environments of woodland and meadow, it was predominantly used for large private estates and public gardens of the time, but the principles can be applied to gardens of all sizes worldwide.

Meadow gardening relies on massed plantings of annuals and perennials. These are chosen to suit the garden's climate and conditions, so that they will thrive, spread and effectively "naturalize." This style allows you to experiment with color and texture on a broader scale and can be extremely rewarding. French artist Claude Monet made meadows in his garden at Giverny, with extensive swathes of flowering annuals and perennials providing him with much inspiration for his art.

MAIN IMAGE: Meadow planting allows plenty of scope for creative expression. In this garden, *Echinacea, Salvia* and *Agapanthus* thrive alongside ornamental grasses, creating an explosion of late summer color.

INSET TOP: This meadow of grasses and delicate flowers is a paradise for chickens and bees.

INSET MIDDLE: An exquisite flower, *Fritillaria meleagris* will naturalize with grasses but prefers cool climates and plenty of moisture.

INSET BOTTOM: Black-eyed Susan (*Rudbeckia hirta*) is a hardy perennial that will spread easily with other meadow plants. Here it creates a sea of yellow against a background of tall golden grasses.

To create a groundcovering meadow or prairie style, it is best to choose plants which are native to your locality or come from similar climates and will readily adapt and naturalize. This ensures that your natural groundcover has a freeflowing look. Perennials can be spread among grass species, and annuals should be allowed to self-seed. While not exactly maintenance-free, once established, a meadow garden can be easily revitalized by reseeding or replanting every year or two.

Ornamental grasses as groundcovers are an essential element of natural styles. They can be used on their own or in mixed drifts with flowering plants to create beautiful meadows and prairies. The great advantage of ornamental grasses is that they provide year-round color and texture, often adding hard-to-find colors, such as silver and brown, and unusual feathery or spiky textures to the garden. Again, grasses which are native to your region, or exotic types suited to the local conditions, are best for natural-style groundcovers; and you can also integrate flowering perennials and annuals with grasslike leaves.

BELOW: A stunning mixed border of ornamental grasses and perennials cascades over a gravel path. The advantage of such a combination is that it will provide year-round interest and creates a complex layering of textures, colors and shapes.

OPPOSITE: *Festuca glauca* forms a tufty blue-green carpet underneath a slender Eucalypt.

## MEADOW FLOWERS

*Crocus tommasinianus* (Crocus)—The slender funnel-shaped crocus flowers pop out of the ground in early spring, followed by their thin leaves. Flowers are pale lilac to dark purple with an orange center. These bulbs are suited to areas with cold winters and hot, dry summers.

*Fritillaria meleagris* (Snake's head fritillaries)—This spring-flowering bulb has slender gray-green leaves and unusual bell-shaped white or purple flowers on fine stems. Can be fussy about conditions, preferring cool climates and moist soil, but will naturalize with grasses.

*Geranium pratense* (Meadow cranesbill)—This hardy clump-forming perennial grows well with grasses in meadows. It has violet-blue flowers in summer.

*Leucojum vernum* (Snowdrop)—These easy-to-grow bulbs flower in early spring, with delicate green-tipped white bells appearing on long stems from clumps of rigid green leaves.

*Myosotis alpestris* (Forget-me-not)—Very easy to grow, the delicate forget-me-not spreads in a carpet of pale blue, pink or white flowers. In the right conditions, it self-seeds freely.

*Narcissus* species and cultivars—All of the *Narcissus* family look wonderful grown in drifts. Jonquils are the earliest flowering and are highly fragrant. There are many varieties, with single or double flowers, from white and pale lemon to the brightest yellow.

*Primula vulgaris* (Common primrose)—Woodland perennials native to the northern hemisphere, the common primrose has single yellow flowers and clumps of furry leaves. Many varieties, in a multitude of colors, derive from this species.

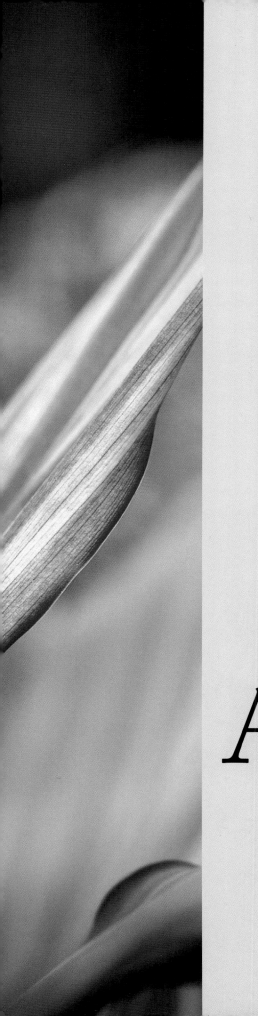

# Architectural
## Details

# ARCHITECTURAL DETAILS

The successful interplay of vertical and horizontal lines in the garden gives it vitality and visual movement, as well as having an important role in creating perspective. A long sweep of lush green lawn will be accentuated and enlivened by an archway at the end of it, perhaps leading to another section of the garden. In much the same way, pyramid-shaped topiaries placed in the corners of a parterre provide relief as well as emphasize the parterre's horizontal lines.

Just as they do in the natural landscape, these continual contrasts and juxtapositions of shape and line in the garden satisfy us visually and aesthetically, and give the garden depth. Architectural details can provide the interplay of height, form and distance by introducing elements such as pergolas, arches or strikingly shaped plants.

RIGHT: This layered *Buxus* hedge adds a strong sense of structure and definition as well as directional movement.

OPPOSITE, CLOCKWISE FROM TOP LEFT: This archway will soon be a tunnel of yellow as laburnum and 'Golden Showers' rose wind their way across the metal supports; a double row of clipped lavender line an avenue and accentuate the focal point and wooden bench; a tunnel of bamboo frames the view and invites further exploration; topiary ivy sentinels mark the division between a paved area and a grassy walkway.

Historically, architectural details such as pergolas, arbors, archways and plant supports have been key elements in garden design, performing both functional and decorative roles. They support plants, and divide sections of the garden. And while plants are the essence of gardens, they alone cannot provide the solid framework that makes a garden design really work—architectural details create bold visual statements and set strong themes.

When planning your garden, consider where it might benefit from architectural elements to bring it to life. Permanent structures like pergolas, formal arbors and other large architectural features need careful planning, as they are integral to the garden's overall design, while metal archways, obelisks and plant-support structures are easily placed and will provide instant results.

TOP: White wisteria cascades from a wooden pergola. Structures such as these bring an important vertical element into the garden and allow climbing plants to be showcased.

MIDDLE: A metal support covered in white *Rosa* 'Helena' creates a romantic arbor over a metal seat.

BOTTOM: This charming children's crawling tunnel has been created by training willow to grow into an arch.

OPPOSITE: A rose covered metal arbor makes a romantic addition to this rambling cottage garden.

## PERGOLAS AND ARBORS

The pergola, like so many of the architectural details we use today, originated in the gardens of ancient Rome. The Roman pergolas were solid structures constructed of stone pillars and timber crossbeams. In a design sense they were used to link the formal architecture of the house to that of the garden, and to provide vertical emphasis in the garden. They also offered protection from the strong Mediterranean sun, creating shady corridors to link areas of the garden and scent-filled arbors for relaxation and reflection.

The perfumed arbors of Medieval pleasure gardens also relied on structural framework to support the heavily intertwined climbing roses and vines, and the construction of the arbor was often decorative in itself. And in the gardens of the Renaissance, supporting trellis and frames provided the backbones of the strongly geometric layout.

Designers such as Gertrude Jekyll and Sir Edwin Lutyens resurrected pergolas in the early twentieth century, using them extensively in their designs. Constructed from local stone and timber, these pergolas performed the same function as those in ancient Roman and Renaissance gardens, visually and thematically linking house and garden, providing vertical emphasis, and acting as a showcase for climbing plants.

BELOW LEFT: The golden autumn foliage of Crimson Glory Vine (*Vitis coignetiae*) makes a spectacular sight in cascading from an Italian-style stone pergola.

BELOW RIGHT: Focal point and linear perspective is given maximum emphasis here – the white vertical path leads that leads the eye to the bench is strongly defined by both the clipped lavender hedges and the rose-covered metal arches.

OPPOSITE: A wisteria-entwined pergola creates an enticing transition between house and garden.

BELOW: A rose arbor covered in the old fashioned rose 'Albertine' makes a beautifully fragrant walkway and frames the view of a stone bust and pedestal.

OPPOSITE: A timber pergola supports a robust *Rosa* 'Cecile Brunner'. Not only does the rose-covered archway create a stunning feature, the contrast of light and shade also adds depth and interest to the garden.

Pergolas have a strong impact on perspective as they work on both the horizontal and vertical planes. A pergola draws you towards a destination, and frames different views of the garden. It also creates two different moods and experiences of the garden—from the outside a pergola invites you in, and on the inside there is a sense of being enclosed and protected.

The pergola's function as a view framer can be effective for creating a focal point. If heavily shaded, the dark tunnel of the pergola will direct the eye to the light beyond, particularly if a feature such as a seat, sculpture or fountain is placed there. It is important that a pergola that acts as an arcade or tunnel should lead somewhere—it could be to another part of the garden, to a decorative feature, or simply to a bench under a tree.

The positioning of the pergola is dependent on its purpose. If it is part of the central axis of the garden or is being used to direct the eye to a focal point, it is likely to be in the center or a prominent part of the garden. If you want to create a vine-covered arbor near the boundary of the garden, you may be able to use the boundary fence or wall to support one side, eliminating the need for one row of supports.

Materials used to construct pergolas vary widely, and what you select will depend on the location of the pergola and the style of your garden. For a formal style you might choose a solid structure of stone and timber; for a romantic-style garden a more open construction using metal might be more appropriate. Sleek modern pergolas can be made using materials such as copper piping or galvanized steel, and elegant tunnels and arcades can be created with intertwined climbers or trained shrubs or trees.

TOP: A tunnel of laburnum creates a magical golden walkway. In the foreground a white *Paeonia suffruticosa* 'Godaishu' is in full bloom.

BOTTOM: A metal pergola covered in grapevine extends the architecture of the house and provides a shady outdoor sitting area.

If located near the house, the pergola should be built of similar materials to that of the building: usually timber or metal, or a combination of brick or stone pillars and timber crossbeams. The dimensions of the pergola should be about 7–8 ft (2.3–2.7 m) in height and 6–8 ft (2–2.7 m) in width, with vertical support posts spaced 6 ft (2 m) apart. The number of crossbeams will affect the amount of shade provided by the pergola. You will need to attach supports such as wire or wire mesh for climbing plants.

When choosing plants to grow over your pergola, picture the desired effect and then select plants which suit both the decorative aim and the growing conditions. For staggered flowering times and year-round interest, choose climbers that flower in different seasons. If you want winter sun and summer shade, deciduous plants are best. Some climbing plants, such as wisteria and bougainvillea, become very woody and heavy after many years, so they will need strong support. Many climbing plants will need regular cutting back to ensure that they do not take over or spread onto nearby structures such as house eaves.

TOP: Perfumed pink roses and wisteria grow in abundance across a timber pergola to form a shady fragrant arbor.

BOTTOM: A curtain of laburnum racemes cascades from a timber pergola, the tunnel of blossoms framing a view of a small statue.

## PLANT SUPPORTS

Supporting structures for climbing and rambling aren't just a practical way to grow plants such as climbing roses, clematis, honeysuckle, jasmine and wisteria, these vertical elements can also act as architectural details in the garden. Plant supports can be as simple as a freestanding wooden pole or a tripod of sticks, or as intricate as an archway constructed of fine metal scrollwork.

Stakes are commonly used for temporarily supporting plants as they establish or flower, and also as permanent supports for standard plants. They are usually made of timber, bamboo or metal. Metal stakes with circular rings at the top allow the plant to grow up through the center and cover the support entirely. They are useful in borders or for creating attractive displays with plants such as standard weeping roses.

A very basic but effective support for fast-growing annual climbers such as sweet peas or beans is a tripod. These can be made using three or more canes of bamboo, stakes or sticks which are tied together at the top. Obelisks are more ornate versions of tripods and can be purchased ready-made, usually in timber or metal, or easily constructed at home. Materials such as willow, wire or wire mesh are easy to work with, and provide ideal plant support.

Simple decorative effects can also be achieved by training climbing plants such as roses onto twisted ropes or wire loops hung between vertical posts, or ivy onto freestanding wire mesh shapes. In fact, your imagination is the limit when it comes to plant supports, and often the most creative solutions are also the most appealing.

ABOVE: A tapered structure of woven willow pieces makes an attractive vertical feature and provides support for climbing plants.

OPPOSITE, CLOCKWISE FROM TOP LEFT: A simple teepee of willow sticks makes a rustic and effective support for sweet peas; bamboo is a light and strong material to use as stakes for these fast growing French beans; an elegantly simple metal and timber device provides support to a peony; these twisted metal spikes are perfect for the growing habit of tomatoes.

The uses for trellis in the garden are endless. It can be used to construct archways, for screens, alongside or on top of fences, for plant support, or as walls for structures like pergolas and summerhouses. Garden designers made extensive use of trellis as far back as the seventeenth century, and illustrations from that era show it used in enclosed cabinets, pergolas, arbors, summerhouses and freestanding supports such as obelisks and pillars.

You can purchase trellis in hardwood or softwood, in square, rectangular or diamond patterns. The panels are also available in a range of shapes and sizes, including curved frames. If you want it to last, it is a good idea to paint or seal the timber, particularly softwood. Hardwood looks good simply varnished or sealed rather than painted, allowing it to retain its natural grain and color.

RIGHT: This robust *Clematis* 'Nelly Moser' makes good use of the painted trellis support behind.

BELOW: A lattice fence becomes a riot of color when the 'American Pillar' rose is in blossom.

OPPOSITE: Trellis attached to a brick wall allows climbing plants such as roses and clematis to clamber easily up the wall. An arch of trellis covered in the climbing rose 'Felicia' gives added emphasis to the brick archway and curved metal gate.

Garden arches and arbors are available ready-made or can be made to order. Metal, while expensive, can look particularly elegant and is worth considering if you want to plant deciduous climbers so that the garden benefits from winter sun. A beautifully made archway of painted ironwork will look attractive as a feature in its own right, even when it is not adorned with climbers.

Sometimes the best support for a climbing plant is another plant. Trees can be put to good use as living support structures, and in nature this is a common sight, with opportunistic vines and rambling plants winding their way around the nearest tree. A rambling rose or wisteria cascading down from the branches of a tree or a clematis twining its way through a hedge makes a wonderful feature. Old fruit trees that are no longer productive also make perfect supports for rambler roses and other climbing plants. Be careful though that the climber does not smother its living host.

It is not only climbing plants that need vertical assistance in the garden. Border plants and herbaceous plants may also require support, especially when first planted. Panels made of woven willow support and protect plants as they become established, and also provide an attractive organic-looking vertical element to borders and garden beds. The panels also make wonderful screens, such as when framed with timber or more contemporary materials such as metal. Even simple wire loops, which can be purchased ready-made to protect borders and control unruly plants, will provide architectural detail for pathways and garden edges.

TOP: A willow-weave pig keeps an unruly herbaceous border in check.

MIDDLE: Simple timber hurdles can be used to keep soft herbaceous plants and borders upright.

BOTTOM: A fine metal arch provides summer support for climbing roses, 'American Pillar' and 'Iceberg' while a straw peacock offers a little support to low growing perennials.

# CLIMBING PLANTS

*Akebia quinata* (Chocolate vine)—A delicate evergreen twining climber with fragrant purple and brown flowers in spring.

*Bougainvillea* species—There are many types of this evergreen, woody-stemmed climber with brilliantly colored flower bracts. Rampant growers, they do best in warm climates and sunny positions and need strong support. Beware of their vicious thorns.

*Clematis armandii*—This species of clematis is a strong-growing, hardy evergreen with fragrant white flowers and dark green leathery leaves. All the Clematis species and cultivars are wonderful plants for walls and pergolas.

*Hydrangea petiolaris* (Climbing hydrangea)—A good structural plant for a partly shaded wall, this deciduous woody-stemmed climber has white flowers in summer.

*Lonicera japonica* (Honeysuckle)—This evergreen twining climber has white tubular flowers that turn honey colored and a long flowering season followed by blackish-blue berries. It will grow in partial shade or full sun.

*Passiflora caerulea* (Passion flower)—This vigorous woody-stemmed tendril climber has attractive flowers in blue, white or pink in summer, and orange fruit in autumn.

*Trachelospermum jasminoides* (Star jasmine)—An evergreen twining climber with attractive foliage that turns bronze in winter, and fragrant white flowers from mid to late summer.

*Vitis vinifera* (Grape vine)—The large, dark green, lobed leaves of the woody-stemmed grape vine turn an attractive red in autumn. The vine's pale green summer flowers are followed by edible fruit.

*Wisteria sinensis* (Chinese wisteria)—This vigorous woody-stemmed deciduous climber has pendant racemes of fragrant lilac or white flowers from mid to late spring.

TOP: A rose covered timber pergola underplanted with lavender creates a fragrant border to this charming timber cottage.

MIDDLE: White wisteria grows across an attractive diamond patterns timber lattice.

BOTTOM: Clematis is a wonderful plant for growing across trellises and garden arches. A rope swag has been attached to the timber pergola to provide further support.

## PLANTS AS ARCHITECTURAL DETAILS

When it comes to architectural elements in the garden, plants allow enormous scope for creativity and imagination. Plants with bold forms or strongly vertical habits, such as ornamental grasses, palms and succulents, can be used as architectural accents. Other plants stand out in a border or bring together a planting scheme because of the color and texture of their foliage or their striking flowers.

Plants can also be shaped and trained into architectural features. The tradition of clipping and molding plant shapes and habits is a long one in both East and West. The hedges and geometric shapes of topiary in Roman and Renaissance gardens gave them form and perspective, just as the beautifully sculpted grass mounds and clipped trees are fundamental to the tranquil mood of Japanese gardens. These techniques still play an important role in modern gardens for the same reasons as in the past—they bring order, add perspective, create focal points and vistas, and provide living ornamentation.

# PLANTS FOR ARCHITECTURAL FORM

Architectural plants are the living sculptures of the garden and will give year-round interest and pleasure. They are chosen for their striking shapes and foliage colors and textures, and can be used as single specimens as focal points or planted in groups for spectacular mass displays.

While some architectural plants, such as the yuccas, oyster plant, globe artichoke and succulents, also have dramatic flowers, most of these plants are chosen for their structural beauty or eye-catching foliage. The distinctive form and foliage of architectural plants such as palms, ferns, cacti, cycads and ornamental grasses make them popular garden features.

The strong look of architectural plants also means they complement hard surfaces and urban settings. When planted near the house, they can help link its architecture with that of the garden. You can use them as focal points in garden beds, or give them even more emphasis in a decorative container. Another advantage of architectural plants is that you often need only one or two to make a statement.

THIS PAGE FROM TOP DOWN: The stiff vertical leaves and striking contrasts of *Yucca gloriosa variegatum*, also known as Spanish dagger, make them popular architectural plants; plants with strong architectural form such as bamboo, *Phormium* and *Melianthus* major work well when grouped together; the sculptural *Eryngium*, commonly known as sea holly, grows up to two metres high and has wonderful gray-green spiky leaves and thistle-like flowers; the delicate foliage and distinctive dark trunk of the Australian tree fern (*Dicksonia antarctica*).

OPPOSITE: The brilliant color of *Canna tropicana* adds a touch of drama.

PAGE 112: A spiral shaped topiary cone makes an interesting feature.

PAGE 113, TOP: The large fan-shaped leaves of Chusan palm (*Trachycarpus fortunei*) add an elegant touch.

PAGE 113, BOTTOM: The spiky leaves of Yucca contrast with the muted tones and textures in this grass garden.

Cacti and succulent plants offer an extraordinarily large range of architectural forms. They are dramatic when planted alone, in groups, or amongst other plant types. A minimalist courtyard spread with white gravel and a single grouping of cacti has a surreal quality and stark beauty. Similarly, succulents in a stone garden are simple but evocative.

Tropical-themed gardens are ideal palettes for architectural plants. A lush and exciting atmosphere can be created by dense plantings, varying color, height and form. Features can be made of palms, cordylines, ferns and bamboo. A striking and contemporary exotic combination could include black bamboo underplanted with ornamental grasses such as fountain grass or black mondo.

Trees with distinctive bark, shape or coloring also make wonderful architectural features. For example, the shimmering bark of the silver birch is spectacular either as a single specimen or when planted in stands, while the sculptural forms of the tortured willow and twisted hazel add their unique elements of drama to the garden.

## ARCHITECTURAL PLANTS

*Acanthus mollis* (Oyster plant)—A striking feature plant, this perennial has large glossy leaves and tall spikes of mauve and white flowers in spring or summer. It prefers partial shade.

*Acer palmatum* (Japanese maple)—This popular species of maple has a compact habit and delicate foliage, bright green in spring, turning brilliant orange, red or yellow in autumn. There are also many cultivars, some with burgundy-colored new foliage or decoratively shaped leaves.

*Agave americana* (Century plant)—With its silvery gray-green fleshy leaves, spiky form and rosette shape, this large succulent is a very popular accent plant in contemporary gardens.

*Astelia* species (Silver spear)—These clump-forming perennials have arching, swordlike silvery leaves that grow to around 4 ft (1.2 m) long.

*Betula pendula* (Birch)—This elegant deciduous tree comes from a large family much favored as ornamental features. Its form, foliage, bark and flowering catkins are all decorative.

*Cordyline* species (Cordyline)—Many types of cordylines are grown for their foliage and form, including the cabbage

tree, *C. australis*, which has long strappy leaves in a starburst habit, and the ti tree, *C. terminalis*, an upright shrub with large broad soft leaves. These cordylines are available with plain green foliage, or as variegated cultivars with cream, pink and red striped leaves.

*Corylus avellana* 'Contorta' (Twisted hazel)—This variety of the cobnut hazel is named for its uniquely twisted stems and branches. It is especially an architectural highlight in winter, when the tree is bare.

*Cynara* species (Artichoke)—The globe artichoke, *C. scolymus*, and its decorative relative the cardoon, *C. cardunculus*, are very useful as feature plants or as accents in herbaceous borders because of their strikingly shaped, silver-gray leaves and dramatic purple flowers.

*Dicksonia antarctica* (Australian tree fern)—This treelike fern has a distinctive brown furry trunk and large glossy green fronds.

*Dracaena sanderiana* (Ribbon plant)—These evergreen tropical shrubs have tall upright canes that bear a fountain of green and white banded leaves.

*Phormium* species and cultivars (New Zealand flax)—These distinctive perennials have stiff, vertical strappy leaves that may be green, bronze or red-purple, in solid colors or striped variegations that can also include pink, red, orange and cream.

*Phyllostachys nigra* (Black bamboo)—This striking, colorful clump-forming bamboo has stems which start off mid-green and mature to a mottled brown and black, contrasting with bright green leaves.

*Salix matsudana* 'Tortuosa' (Tortured willow)—A variety of willow which has twisted and contorted stems and branches enhanced by a tall, narrow habit; an outstanding architectural feature.

*Trachycarpus fortunei* (Chusan palm)—This slow-growing palm features a broad crown of large fan-shaped leaves on a stout trunk.

*Yucca* species (Yucca)—An amazing group of plants, yuccas make bold accents in the garden. Popular species include the Spanish dagger, *Y. gloriosa*, which has rosettes of sharp pointed green leaves, and Adam's needle, *Y. filamentosa*, which has swordlike leaves edged with tangled threadlike strands.

LEFT: The dramatic spiky leaves of Agave *americana* 'Marginata'.

OPPOSITE, LEFT: An interplay of texture and form with Agave and cactus.

OPPOSITE, RIGHT: Yuccas planted in a bed of black mondo grass make a dramatic feature.

# TOPIARY

Topiary, the art of clipping plants to form ornamental shapes and patterns, can be seen at its most sophisticated in the grand designs and clipped formality of the French gardens of the seventeenth and eighteenth centuries. Even today the French continue the craft on a large scale in their public gardens and parks.

For most people, topiary is a useful tool to bring definition or an element of whimsy to the garden. The average garden of today is not large, so there is little point trying to reproduce the ornate parterres and topiaries of Versailles. Having said that, there is really no limit to what shape can be created, and the many gardens dotted with all manner of eccentrically clipped creatures and objects are a testament to the creative use of topiary. In a design sense, though, topiary works best when used sparingly, to create focus points or punctuation marks in the garden.

Hedging is familiar across all cultures and this popular form of plant clipping goes hand-in-hand with topiary. Hedges can be punctuated by a series of windows, arches or topiary shapes such as columns, parapets, obelisks and pyramids. Topiary screens of regularly spaced matching shapes, such as ball-top standards, make an interesting and more open alternative to a solid hedge.

BELOW: A fragrant 'living' seat makes a wonderfully textured feature with its mix of clipped hedge back and arms, ivy-covered front and scented chamomile seat.

OPPOSITE, CLOCKWISE FROM TOP LEFT: A topiary bunny rests on the lawn bringing a touch of whimsy to a formal garden; these tiny clipped pyramids are part of a miniature topiary forest; hornbeams clipped into lollipop shapes stand out in vivid contrast to the deep purple of the prunus hedge and lush green lawn; topiary balls punctuate a perennial border.

Topiary is not a technique for the impatient, as most of the favored plants for topiary are slow growing. Evergreen hedging plants such as yew, box, bay or privet are commonly used (see page 63). It may be ten years before the final result is achieved, but there is much satisfaction along the way. And if planted in a container, a topiary still working towards its final shape can be taken with you if you have to move. Of course, you can also purchase completed topiary, usually in the form of cones, pyramids, balls and standards, for instant results.

Geometric topiary shapes work particularly well in small gardens and can be used to flank a pathway, to highlight an entrance or steps, or as architectural features. Less formal shapes can bring an individual flavor to the garden, reflecting a theme or echoing a shape from elsewhere in the garden or from the architecture of the house. The other advantage of using topiary for the small garden, especially when combined with formal hedging or parterres, is that it provides year-round interest and structure.

Cloud topiary, which is popular in formal gardens of China and Japan, is like a cross between bonsai and topiary. Highly original shapes are created by severely clipping shrubs or trees to expose the branches, leaving foliage "clouds" on the upper side and ends of branches. The result is very evocative and sculptural, the plants resembling wind-ravaged mature trees.

TOP: Frost-covered topiary lollipops with tufted bases line the edge of water channel.

bottom: An ornate antique planter box is decorated with clipped topiary and an ivy garland.

OPPOSITE: The sculptural and evocative effect of cloud topiary is shown here in this sculpted *Ilex crenata* (Japanese holly). By selectively clipping the tree, the limbs are exposed and the foliage formed into cloud-like shapes on the upper sides of the branches.

# ESPALIER AND OTHER FORMS OF TRAINING

The training of plants to grow in one plane or in a particular shape has a long history. In courtyard gardens it enables plants which would otherwise be too large to be controlled and confined to the space. On a grander scale, such as in the avenues of pleached lime trees so commonly seen in French landscapes, it is used to create perspective and to lead the eye to the vista beyond.

Through methods such as espalier and pleaching it is possible to train plants to grow into highly stylized patterns. This can be used to great effect to establish strongly defined vertical and horizontal axes through multiple plantings or rows of trained plants.

Standards and pollarding techniques create plants with distinctive and decorative shapes. These forms of training are particularly suited to confined urban gardens, where the ultimate size of many shrubs and trees means they cannot be freely grown. Standards are especially favored as contemporary garden details, in both formal and natural styles.

BELOW: An espaliered pear tree grows along wire supports to spectacular effect.

OPPOSITE, CLOCKWISE FROM TOP LEFT: Fruit trees such as apple, pear, plum, apricots and cherries are all ideal for espalier; espaliered camellia has been trained in a criss-cross pattern on either side of a dense arch of *Ficus pumila*; fruit trees can be trained onto a frame to form interesting shapes – here a pear tree has been grown into a decorative tripod shape; plants are trained along horizontal wires on a high wall.

While espalier takes some effort and there is a long wait for the final results, it is not a difficult technique and the effects of training plants on a single plane can be quite spectacular. To espalier a tree you will need a support frame or wall to which wires are attached in evenly spaced parallel horizontal lines, usually around 18 inches (45 cm) apart. As the tree grows, its branches are trained along the support wires. Fruit trees such as apples, pears, plums, apricots and cherries are all ideal for this treatment.

Other common patterns for espalier include fan shape, cordon and U-shape. For a fan shape, branches are trained upwards and outwards from a single point near the base of the main stem. For a cordon, a single stem is trained along a support either vertically or at an angle. You can also create a variety of U-shapes by training the branches outwards and upwards on either side of the main stem. These espalier shapes can be planted in groups for a massed effect; as they take up very little space, they are also ideal for small gardens, either for screening or as a feature against a wall.

RIGHT: A cherry tree espaliered into a fan shape by training the branches upwards and outwards from the base creates a spectacular feature on this painted brick wall.

BELOW: A thornless blackberry has been trained into graceful arches along a wooden fence to make a living, edible boundary to a vegetable garden.

Standards are great features that add a vertical element or focal point to the garden, and also save space. Most trees and shrubs can be trained as standards, with a single main stem topped by foliage which may be shaped into a ball or naturally cascading. To train a plant as a standard, prune the lower branches are regularly pruned so that the stem remains bare and the foliage is encouraged to grow on top.

Pleaching is a great way to create a leafy screen for summer, and the symmetry and regularity of the intertwined branches is also attractive when the trees are without leaf in the colder months. Usually applied to broad-leaved trees, pleaching involves severely pruning the lower part of the plant so that foliage is restricted to the top, usually on one plane. It is also used to create avenues and alleys, either with the branches trained horizontally so that they intertwine or with the trees cut into box shapes. The most commonly used tree for pleaching is the lime or linden, and these work well when clipped into box, rectangular or rounded shapes. Pleaching can also be used to create a hedge that looks as if it is on stilts, with the bare trunks lined up at regular intervals beneath the clipped foliage.

Pollarding is a rather extreme method of pruning trees so that knots or knobs develop at the ends of the branches. The main branches are cut back regularly, permanently stunting their growth so that the ends of the branches develop a distinctive knobbly and swollen appearance. While severe, pollarding can be used to create interesting sculptural-looking plants.

BELOW: The formal air of this avenue of *Sorbis aria* 'Lutescens' has been created by pruning the lower part of each plant.
OPPOSITE: These standard holly trees with their pruned lollipop shape and sharp leaves add a visual contrast to the softness of the lavender below.

# Sensory
## Details

# SENSORY DETAILS

The mood of your garden is influenced by many factors—the design and style, the materials used and its location and climate—but it is the sensory details that really influence the way you will respond to it. Color, texture, scent and taste are the essential ingredients that give the garden vitality and atmosphere. These are the elements which really determine its mood, which can be formal, abstract, natural, contemporary or romantic.

Plants stimulate the senses in the garden. Some provide color and texture in flowers and foliage, others bring fragrance or flavor. Plants also work on a deeper sensory level, reaching out to our emotions. This is particularly true of scent, which can have a potent effect on our emotions and moods, sometimes stimulating memories and triggering a response that we may not understand. It is the essential oils of plants that give them their specific scent and we have been extracting these oils for thousands of years to use in religious and cultural ceremonies, for medicinal use and to manufacture perfumes.

The effect of color on mood is also well recognized, with whole industries built around designing color schemes to induce particular responses. In the garden, the effect is immediate, the cool shades such as blues and greens having a soothing effect and the hotter shades such as orange and red creating a sense of excitement and drama.

Texture is not only visually satisfying, it also brings a tactile element into your garden. It is hard to resist touching any highly textured surface and plants are no exception. The juxtaposition of foliage shape and textures—smooth against rough, sharp and pointed against soft and downy—is enticing.

Add to the mix some edible plants such as fruit trees, herbs or vegetables and you may never want to leave the sensory paradise you have created.

TOP: The vibrant colors of *Cordyline* catch the eye in this predominantly green tropical garden.

BOTTOM: The large heart-shaped leaves of *Hosta* 'Wide Brim,' with their wonderful lime green borders, cut a swathe of color and texture through the garden.

OPPOSITE: A curtain of yellow laburnum cascades over an arbor, forming a sensational backdrop to a border of purple *Allium* 'Purple Sensation' and yellow *Iris* 'Jeanne Price'.

## COLOR

Color is a powerful element in the garden. It can be used to create mood, to highlight certain areas, and to provide a sense of perspective and depth in the garden. Bright or hot colors add drama and bring the highlighted area or object into the foreground. Soft, muted colors, on the other hand, blur boundaries and let the eye move onwards towards a more clearly defined object or area of the garden. You can make use of this effect to have certain areas appear wider or longer and to direct the eye away from less attractive sections.

Color, both in plants and materials, will determine the style of garden and the mood you create. Romantic, soft pastels and accent plants of silver-gray and deep green will create a serene mood, while a feature wall in vibrant blue or pink offset with architectural plants such as agave or cacti is electrifying. In a Mediterranean-style garden, strong earthy and pinkish terracotta tones of buildings and plant containers are complemented by silver-gray foliage of olive trees, lavender and santolina.

It is useful to look to talented garden designers of the past and present for inspiration in the use of color. In the color-themed garden "rooms" designed by Vita Sackville-West and the intricately planned perennial borders of Gertrude Jekyll, color was the essence of the garden. Monet created an artist's paradise in his garden at Giverny, the creative plant and color combinations still inspiring designers and gardeners to this day.

Vita Sackville-West is widely regarded as the greatest plantswoman of her time. Her expert use of color and plant combinations is apparent in the series of rooms at Sissinghurst, her garden in England. The "White Garden," where all the flowers are white and the foliage gray, is probably the most famous: box hedges border garden beds containing a profusion of white flowers such as snapdragons, crambe and nicotiana, with silver or gray foliage plants like artemisia, and 'Iceberg' roses underplanted with white pulmonarias.

TOP: A predominantly white garden is given greater depth with the addition of purple and gray highlights.

BOTTOM: The aqua-blue of the pond is brought out in sharp relief against the complementary tone of the purple wall.

Gertrude Jekyll, who trained as an artist, revealed a deep understanding of the use of color and texture to create mood and perspective in the garden. In the perennial borders she designed, Jekyll used pastel-colored flowers mixed with foliage of gray and dusty blue-green, and sophisticated combinations of cloudy and spiky plants. Bright colors were used as highlights, dotted through the garden to direct vision and create movement.

In Monet's garden at Giverny in France the vibrant mix of colors and unusual combinations provided him with year-round material for his paintings. The water gardens, with their winding pathways, gracefully arched bridges and abundance of waterlilies, have a serene and soothing atmosphere of pastels, blues and greens, while the tumbling display of vibrant colors in the nasturtium walk is stimulating and cheerful.

In his minimalist gardens, Mexican architect and landscape designer Luis Barragan made dramatic use of color for spatial effect and to create mood. Walls are a central feature of Barragan's designs, forming intense blocks of color that act as focal points and creators of mood. Hot colors such as bright pink are intensified through texture and contrasted with cool elements such as water. Features such as long narrow water channels or rills, lined with black tiles or rock so that they reflect the sky, are punctuated at the end by a vibrant blue wall. Barragan used blue walls as metaphors for the sky and yellow to create the warmth of sunlight.

Contemporary naturalist designers Wolfgang Oehme and James van Sweden, working in the United States, display sophisticated understanding of the interplay of color, texture and pattern in their natural-looking but carefully planned borders of perennials and grasses.

TOP: The use of blue to color the retaining walls gives greater emphasis to the bronze *Cordyline*.

BELOW: This golden border is rich and varied in both texture and color. The graduated tones of yellow, orange and red dahlias intermingle with a soft haze of fennel flowers and grasses.

# PLANTS FOR COLOR

## Silver and blue-gray foliage

*Artemisia* 'Powis Castle' (Wormwood)—An aromatic, softly textured evergreen perennial with silver-gray foliage; it needs plenty of sun.

*Brachyglottis* species (Dusty miller)—These mound-forming evergreen shrubs are sometimes known as *Senecio*. Grown for their silver-edged distinctively shaped leaves, most also have golden-yellow daisylike flowers.

*Festuca glauca* (Blue fescue)—Growing to about 18 inches (45 cm ) in height, this tufty evergreen perennial has thin, grasslike, gray-blue leaves.

*Helichrysum italicum* (Curry plant)—An evergreen small shrub with aromatic silvery-green leaves and yellow flowers.

*Lavandula* species (Lavender)—Grown for both the silver-gray leaves and fragrant flowers, these evergreen perennials prefer sunny positions and do not like to be overwatered. The foliage may be clipped, either for light shaping or in low hedges.

*Rosmarinus officinalis* (Rosemary)—This evergreen shrub has highly aromatic leaves which are also used for cooking. There are many cultivars, with blue, purple, pink or white flowers; the taller ones are ideal for borders, and low-growing forms are good for edging.

*Salvia officinalis* (Common sage)—This culinary sage has aromatic felt-like gray-green leaves and purple flowers.

*Santolina chamaecyparissus* (Cotton lavender)—Also sometimes called santolina, this evergreen perennial's delicate silvery-green leaves look great in a mixed border. It has buttonlike yellow flowerheads on long stems.

*Stachys byzantina* (Lamb's ears)—The furry, large, green-gray leaves of this easy-growing evergreen perennial make an effective contrast with green foliage in a border.

## White and cream flowers

*Digitalis purpurea* f. *alba* (White foxglove)—A biennial with a tall spike of white tubular-shaped flowers rising from a large rosette of leaves.

*Gardenia augusta*—Popular for their rich green, glossy leaves and highly perfumed flowers, these evergreen shrubs prefer a hot summer and plenty of water.

*Helleborus orientalis* (Lenten rose)—Great for shady spots or part-shade, such as under deciduous trees, this evergreen perennial has cupped white and pink flowers in winter.

*Lilium* species—This extensive family of plants includes many famous white flowers, such as the popular and fragrant oriental lily, *L. regale*; the Christmas or November lily, *L. longiflorum*; and the Madonna lily, *L. candidum*.

*Rosa* 'Iceberg'—The white-flowered 'Iceberg' is one of the most popular and hardiest of the roses, and flowers prolifically when in a good, sunny position.

*Zantedeschia aethiopica* (Arum lily)—A tuberous perennial with funnel-shaped pure white flowers on long, elegant stems in spring. This architectural plant has large, broad leaves, and is fond of damp conditions.

OPPOSITE, CLOCKWISE FROM TOP LEFT: The purity and crispness of white orchids; the blue-gray spiky leaves and thistle-like flowers of *Eryngium*, commonly known as sea holly, makes it a wonderful addition to a perennial border; Alyssum produces a carpet of white in the Spring garden and is a hardy plant for borders and rock gardens; *Stachys byzantina*, with its soft downy leaves and mauve flower spikes, is a popular and attractive plant for blue-gray highlights.

## Red and pink flowers

*Anigozanthos manglesii* (Kangaroo paw)—From Western Australia, this tuft-forming perennial makes a great feature plant with its sword-shaped leaves and unique vivid red and green flowers on tall spikes. Dislikes frosts and summer humidity.

*Dahlia* cultivars (Dahlia)—The dazzling colors of dahlias include many striking reds and pinks, as well as softer tones and multicolored blooms. Flowers range from single forms to fully double or ornamental, such as the cacti-flowered dahlia and pompom.

*Echinacea purpurea* (Purple coneflower)—This easy-to-grow perennial has tall stems of large daisylike flowers with bright pink petals and a prominent dark center.

*Kniphofia caulescens* (Red-hot poker)—This striking evergreen perennial from southern Africa has arching grasslike leaves and a long spire packed with red flowers.

*Monarda didyma* (Bergamot)—A tall summer-flowering perennial with masses of fragrant flowers in scarlet, carmine, rose-pink or pink on long stems. The blooms attract honeyeating birds and butterflies.

*Papaver orientale* (Oriental poppy)—This perennial poppy has a range of flower colors which includes shades of striking red to pale pink; the flowers often have a large distinctive black spot on each petal.

*Pelargonium* species and cultivars (Pelargonium)—There are many varieties of this very popular perennial, and they include an extensive palette of reds and pinks as well as bicolors, striped petals and other unusual markings.

*Penstemon* cultivars (Penstemon)—A favorite of the flower border, this perennial has tall stems of tubular flowers. There are many cultivars, including colors from deep dark red and magenta to pastel pink.

*Sedum spectabile* (Ice plant)—The long-lasting flowers, ranging in color from pale pink through to dark mauve-pink, on these succulent perennials make them very useful for color. They are easy to grow and suit both architectural gardens and flower borders.

## Yellow and orange flowers

*Calendula officinalis* (Marigold)—These classic yellow flowers are available in the common single-petaled form as well as doubles, in tones from pale gold to deep orange. Very easy to grow, these annuals flower profusely from spring to autumn.

*Clivia miniata* (Clivia)—This shade-loving perennial has dark green strappy leaves and brilliant orange flowers in winter.

*Coreopsis* species and cultivars (Coreopsis)—These easy-to-grow annuals and perennials have a profusion of rich yellow, daisylike flowers throughout summer. They thrive in full sun and are fairly tolerant of drought.

*Eschscholzia californica* (Californian poppy)—This fast-growing and free-flowering annual has bright yellow and orange flowers and fernlike leaves. It looks particularly good in drifts.

*Helianthus annuus* (Sunflower)—These annuals are famous for their golden-yellow flowers. The tall varieties make striking accents when in bloom, though they may need staking.

*Strelitzia reginae* (Bird-of-paradise flower)—This wonderful architectural feature plant has bright orange flowers on long rigid stems, resembling a bird's head. These evergreen perennials form large clumps, and are drought-resistant but also like the tropics.

*Tagetes* species and cultivars (African or French marigold)—These profusely flowering annuals bring vibrant color, ranging from yellow-gold to deep red. The taller varieties are ideal for flower beds, while the smaller types are perfect for edging.

OPPOSITE, CLOCKWISE FROM TOP LEFT: *Hippeastrums* come in a range of bright colors including this wonderful red with contrasting brilliant yellow stamen; *Echinacea purpureum* is a showy addition to the pink and yellow border and it comes complete with complementary contrasting yellow center; the hot colors of this yellow Daylily 'Corky' and red *Crocosmia* 'Lucifer' add some drama to the garden; the daisy-like *Hellenium* is a hardy plant that comes in a range of orange and brown tones.

ABOVE: There is nothing quite like the sweet pea for both color and fragrance. Modern hybrids come in an enormous range of colors and produce more flowers to a stem.

OPPOSITE, CLOCKWISE FROM TOP LEFT: A useful plant for growing in either containers or garden beds, *Anagallis monelli's* sky blue flowers work well with white or yellow companions; *Agapanthus africanus* are favorites around the world for their dramatic starbursts of blue or white flowers; *Campanula carpatica*, with its delicate mauve bell-shaped flowers is a popular plant for the blue palette; the bright blue of *Ajuga reptans* harmonizes perfectly with the soft blue-gray of *Echeveria*.

## Blue and purple flowers

*Agapanthus* species (Agapanthus)—These clump-forming perennials make great architectural plants with their strappy dark green leaves and long stems of tubular blue and mauve flowers.

*Convolvulus mauritanicus* (Ground morning glory)—This trailing perennial with soft lavender-blue flowers is a popular groundcover. It needs full sun to flower well.

*Echium fastuosum* (Pride of Madeira)—This evergreen shrub has large upright panicles of purple flowers and a striking densely branched habit of gray-green leaves which makes it ideal as an architectural or accent plant.

*Lavandula* species and cultivars—These evergreen perennials are famous for their fragrant purple-blue flowers, though they are also available in white and pink tones.

*Meconopsis betonicifolia* (Himalayan blue poppy)—This delicate perennial has highly desirable pure blue poppylike flowers. It can be tricky to grow, and is only suitable for moist conditions in cool and cold climates.

*Nepeta* species (Catmint)—These hardy perennials have fragrant, attractive gray foliage and mauve flower spikes; they look great when mass planted, and low-growing types are especially suited to edging.

*Salvia* species (Sage)—This large family of plants includes many species with purple or blue flowers, such as mealy sage, *S. farinacea*; *S. pratensis*, with royal blue flowers; and *S. uliginosa*, with turquoise-colored blooms.

*Veronica* species and cultivars (Speedwell)—These perennials have tall flower spikes in summer that bear blue, mauve or pink flowers. There are low-growing, spreading forms, ideal for groundcover, as well as taller types suitable for drifts and flower beds.

# TEXTURE

Texture, like color, brings the garden to life and reveals its very essence and personality. In a formal garden based on classical lines, texture plays a dominant role, as success relies on varying shades of green and interplays of foliage. For example, clipped hedges of box, yew or other glossy-leafed evergreens contrast well with silver-gray and velvety-textured foliage such as lamb's ear, cotton lavender, dusty miller and lavender.

Where space is limited, texture can be used to great effect, and can also give a sense of wider boundaries. For example, in a gravel-covered courtyard a single group of spiky yuccas planted against a wall of vibrant blue or deep terracotta makes an elegant statement rich in connotations of hot climates and open spaces. Ornamental grasses planted in swathes and leading down to a sandy-edged rock pool paint a highly textured picture and also evoke the mood of a natural landscape setting.

The textures of other materials such as walls, paving, ornaments and furniture also add to the garden's mood. The roughness of old bricks and cobblestones is enhanced when interspersed with spiky mondo grass or mounds of springy moss, while sandstone edging perfectly contrasts with a lush green lawn.

RIGHT: The downy leaves of *Artemisia* give it a soft glow, making it an invaluable plant for silver highlights. The distinctive, clearly defined shape of its leaves also adds structural form and texture to borders.

OPPOSITE, CLOCKWISE FROM TOP LEFT: This richly textured mix creates a visual feast with the deep red velvet of Sedum 'Autumn Joy' standing out in sharp relief from a hazy background of *Panicum* seed heads. In front, *Artemisia* provides a downy silver glow and bronze-leaved Canna echoes the red tones to the side; yellow knobbly spears of *Kniphofia* are accompanied by the bright bobbing heads of sunflowers against a background of soft green foliage. In the foreground is the deep bronze of *Berberis*; this beautiful composition combines the balled pink flowers of Sedum with the feathery panicles of *Pennisetum alopecuroides* 'Woodside' (fountain grass) and the soft reddish-bronze haze of *Panicum virgatum*, commonly known as switch grass; the spear like heads and strappy purple-bronze leaves of *Pennisetum* 'Purple Majesty' bring a dynamic element to a perennial border.

Plants with silver or gray leaves gain their distinctive appearance from a covering of fine hairs on their foliage. This creates a silvery haze reminiscent of hot climates and evokes the mood of the Mediterranean, the desert and other arid locales. Many of the silver-gray plants also have attractive flowers, but they are mostly grown for their outstanding foliage, which brings color and texture to the garden year-round.

The architectural plants with dramatic form and foliage—such as cacti, succulents, palms and ornamental grasses—also provide a great deal of texture in the garden. They can be used to wonderful effect as features in single plantings, in groups, or mixed and contrasted with other plants.

Plants valued for their tactile qualities should be introduced to the garden wherever possible. Include trees with interesting bark, such as the broadleaf paperbark, silver birch, paper-bark maple, palms and many of the Prunus family. Ornamental grasses with their feathery seedheads and strappy leaves are irresistible to the touch, as are the velvety leaves of lamb's ear and lavender and the rounded smoothness of plants such as succulents.

# ORNAMENTAL GRASSES

*Carex elata* (Tufted sedge)—An evergreen low-growing perennial that forms a grasslike clump and is perfect for underplanting and for borders. The very popular variety 'Aurea' is commonly called Bowles' golden sedge and has bright yellow-green leaves.

*Cortaderia selloana* (Pampas grass)—This perennial grass forms a large clump that makes it an ideal accent plant. The tall, feathery, silvery-white plumes emerge in summer and remain decorative through autumn and winter. The cultivar 'Pumila' has broad, fluffy white seedheads, while 'Sunningdale Silver' is more feathery and silver.

*Elmyus hispidis* (Wheatgrass)—Attractive spiky green leaves with finely pointed seedheads.

*Festuca glauca* (Blue fescue)—This evergreen perennial grass is popular for its compact tufts of blue-green leaves; ideal as edging for borders and paving.

*Helictotrichon sempervirens* (Blue oat grass)—A striking evergreen perennial grass forming tufts of stiff gray-blue leaves; it is hardy, and also tolerates dry conditions.

*Miscanthus sinensis* (Japanese silver grass)—A decorative addition to mixed borders, this perennial grass forms great clumps and has feathery flowerheads in summer; 'Variegatus' has blue-green leaves striped with cream, 'Zebrinus' has leaves with horizontal cream stripes, and 'Gracillimus' has soft gray-green foliage.

*Ophiopogon* species (Mondo grass)—Among the most popular of grasslike perennials, these include the common mondo, *O. japonicus*, which is available in tall and short forms, and the black mondo, *O. planiscapus* 'Nigrescens'.

*Pennisetum* species (Fountain grass)—Many species of this perennial grass are grown ornamentally. They feature fine, soft feathery panicles that often last well into winter.

*Stipa* species (Feather grass)—This group of ornamental grasslike perennials includes the pheasant's tail grass, *S. arundinacea*, an evergreen with arching orange-brown leaves, and the giant feather grass, *S. gigantea*, which has flowerheads that stand high above the leaves on long, thin stems.

ABOVE: A massed planting of *Stipa gigantea* creates a tall border beside stone steps.

OPPOSITE, CLOCKWISE FROM TOP LEFT: *Carex selata* (tufted sedge) is perfect for low borders; *Festuca glauca* has distinctive blue-green leaves and long fine stalks; the fine feathery flower heads of *Miscanthus*; clumps of *Miscanthus* create a softly mounded border.

PAGE 142, TOP LEFT: This yellow and blue combination contrasts the soft feathery texture of *Stipa* with the thistle-like spikiness of *Eryngium*.

PAGE 142, TOP RIGHT: The delicate silvery leaves of *Santolina* make it a perfect choice for this border where it has been clipped into rounded mounds to provide an edging for lavender.

PAGE 142, BOTTOM: The rich mahogany and distinctive peeling bark of *Prunus serrula* (Tibetan cherry) adds a wonderful tactile element to the garden.

PAGE 143: The wonderful juxtaposition of the sharply pointed leaves of the *Doryanthes excelsa*, commonly known as Gymea Lily, and the feathery panicles of *Miscanthus sinensis*.

## SCENT

Scent is integral to the experience of the garden. It creates mood, stimulates as well as soothes, and adds a sensual dimension to your garden.

Scent also attracts all sorts of birds and insects that play their part in pollinating and spreading the seeds of plants. Having a wide variety of species of perfumed plants in your garden will ensure an active community of birds and insects. And there is nothing quite as intoxicating on a hot summer's night as the sweet scent of a plant releasing its fragrance to attract moths and other nocturnal creatures.

When planning a scented garden, place perfumed plants close to the house and entertaining areas. Jasmine, wisteria and fragrant climbing roses are perfect for growing over a pergola or arbor. For an unbeatable evening fragrance, try the Arabian jasmine, which has delicate sprays of sweetly scented flowers. Scented feature shrubs could include Chinese witch hazel and gardenias; orange jessamine makes a wonderful perfumed hedge; or for background planting, try pittosporum or mock orange. Pockets of fragrant groundcovers planted in amongst paving or along the edges of pathways release delicious aromas when crushed underfoot, as does a chamomile or thyme lawn.

Scented plants are ideal for feature pots, which can be used to perfume balconies, courtyards and roof gardens. In pots, these plants can also be moved around so that you can best enjoy their fragrances. Herbs such as lavender, thyme and rosemary will thrive in pots, as will pelargoniums, some of which have strongly scented leaves.

TOP: This shaded arbor is filled with the heady scent of *Wisteria sinensis* right throughout summer.

BOTTOM: A hedged herb garden contains a wonderful blend of aromas from the pungent scent of lavender to the distinctive fragrance of thyme, curry plant (*Helichrysum italicum*) and winter savory (*Satureia montana*).

OPPOSITE: This courtyard, filled with the scent of pelargoniums and roses, is a fragrant retreat.

# FRAGRANT PLANTS

*Brugmansia suaveolens* (Angel's trumpet)—The enormous trumpet-shaped white flowers on this shrub add the most delicious fragrance to the garden in summer.

*Jasminum* species (Jasmine)—This climber comes in many types and, depending on the species, has wonderfully fragrant yellow, white or pink flowers. The common jasmine, *J. polyanthum*, with abundant white flowers, bursts into bloom at the first sign of spring. Arabian jasmine, *J. sambac*, has intensely sweet flowers that resemble tiny creamy-white roses, and blooms in spring, summer and autumn.

*Lavandula* species and cultivars (Lavender)—Both the silver-gray foliage and the flowers of these popular perennials are aromatic, although the flowers are more valuable commercially. For the best fragrance, choose varieties which are grown for the perfume industry.

*Lonicera* species (Honeysuckle)—The fragrant honey-filled flowers of this pretty shrub attract birds, bees and children to the garden.

*Murraya paniculata*—This attractive evergreen shrub has glossy dark green leaves and strongly scented white flowers. It likes a semishaded position and makes a wonderful fragrant hedge.

*Philadelphus coronarius* (Mock orange)—This deciduous shrub has masses of white flowers in summer; these appear in clusters and have an intense orange-blossom fragrance.

*Pittosporum* species—These evergreen trees and shrubs are grown for both their ornamental foliage year-round and their strongly perfumed cream flowers in spring; in some types these may be followed by decorative orange berries.

*Rosa* cultivars (Rose)—This most popular of flowers comes in an enormous number of species and hybrids but not all are highly perfumed. Check with your local nursery for the best scented roses for your location.

*Wisteria sinensis* (Chinese wisteria)—This strong twining climber has racemes of fragrant purple flowers; there is also a white-flowering variety. It can be trained to create scented arbors and pergolas, or grown as a standard.

BELOW LEFT: *Philadelphus* 'Belle Etoile' is one of the several varieties of mock orange, all of which have an intense orange blossom fragrance.

BELOW RIGHT: The pungent aroma of lavender comes from the oils in both the flower heads and the leaves.

OPPOSITE: The modern hybrid rose *Rosa* 'Constance Spry' combines a vigorous growing habit with old-fashioned style and fragrance. The large pink blooms have an evocative spicy perfume.

## EDIBLE PLANTS

Kitchen gardens, once the staple of gardens around the world, have made a comeback and are often incorporated into even the smallest of contemporary gardens. There is something quite magical about kitchen gardens—not only are herbs, vegetables and fruit trees just as beautiful as ornamental plants, but growing them to feed your household can be deeply satisfying.

Kitchen and medicinal gardens have a long and colorful history. In Medieval Europe formal kitchen gardens were located close to the main buildings and contained a mix of common vegetables and medicinal herbs. In the sixteenth century the French perfected the potager, or kitchen garden, dedicating large areas to geometric garden beds edged with clipped hedges. Villandry, a showpiece of the Renaissance French potager, is a testament to the stunning beauty and extensive range of edible plants grown both in the sixteenth century and today. Located on the banks of the Loire River in France, Villandry has a series of kitchen gardens planted out with absolute precision and including a rich variety of vegetables, fruits and herbs.

BELOW LEFT: Herbs are not only edible, they are decorative and wonderfully fragrant. Here, the yellow flowers of curry plant (*Helichrysum italicum*) complement the mauve shades of several varieties of thyme.

BELOW RIGHT: Silverbeet, runner beans and onions thrive in this luscious vegetable garden.

OPPOSITE: This vegetable garden is a sensual delight with its richly textured display. In the foreground lettuce creates a vivid green border to the long pointed leaves and fluffy pink flower heads of chives.

Such gardens are an inspiration to modern gardeners, but for most of us, without a team of laborers on hand, an extensive kitchen garden is simply not possible. A great deal can be achieved, though, even in a tiny courtyard. Vegetables and herbs can be grown in their own beds or mixed with other plants. If there is no space for garden beds, planter boxes, pots and other containers can be used for herbs and vegetables, even on balconies.

The traditional layout used by Medieval monastic "herbers," where edible and medicinal plants were grown in raised beds and laid out in geometric patterns, can be particularly effective in small gardens or courtyards. The raised beds can be made of brick, timber or woven willow. Alternatively, leave the beds at ground level and define them with box hedges or gravel paths.

For a Mediterranean-style garden, a grapevine-covered pergola creates a productive and decorative summer bower. Citrus trees such as lemon, lime, mandarin and orange can be grown either in the garden beds or in large containers. Aromatic herbs such as rosemary, lavender, thyme and oregano, grown as borders close to the house, can be readily picked for use in the kitchen.

TOP: Vegetables grow happily alongside perennials in this colorful mixed garden bed.

BOTTOM: Rows of cabbages and lettuce create a colorful tapestry.

Fruit trees are a delight in any garden, for their fruit, beautiful form and blossoms. They can be espaliered against a wall or fence or trained to form a screen around the edge of your kitchen garden. For a spectacular effect, create a fruit-tree tunnel by training apple or pear trees over a supportive archway. You will need to use two-year-old apple or pear trees on semidwarfing rootstocks and plant the trees about 2–3 ft (60–90 cm) apart. This is a long-term project and will require vigilant pruning to ensure good growth but it will be very rewarding when completed, creating a shady, productive and fragrant arbor.

A mixed garden of perennials and edible plants is also very rewarding and some unusual combinations can be achieved. Sweet peas can be grown on frames or onto fences alongside colorful runner beans; fruit trees such as fig, nectarine, peach and apple can be trained against a sunny wall; and archways can be draped with grapevines and wisteria. Herbs will happily grow in an ornamental border alongside cutting flowers, their seedheads adding interest and texture when flowers are scarce.

Many edible plants are also striking accent plants. The cardoon, a relative of the artichoke, with its spiky foliage and purple thistlelike flowers, is a great addition to the perennial border. Vegetables such as cabbages, chard and the onion family add interesting colors, shapes and textures, while gourds and marrows have highly decorative leaves, vibrant flowers and extravagant fruit.

TOP: Rainbow silverbeet, the result of cross breeding to produce a range of richly colored stalks, is sweeter and more delicate in flavor than plain silverbeet and makes a colorful and nutritious addition to the vegetable garden.

BOTTOM: Scarlet zinnia color co-ordinates with the bright stems of rainbow silverbeet.

# Water

# WATER

Volatile, shifting and reflective, water is the ultimate mood creator, and can change the entire focus of the garden. It can be used for dramatic effect or, equally, to create a soothing, contemplative atmosphere.

Water has been a dominant feature of garden designs throughout history. The ancient Romans used sophisticated systems of hydraulics in their formal gardens to pump water into courtyard pools and fountains, as well as to saunas and bath houses. In Renaissance gardens water was put to great use as a key design element, with ponds, pools and fountains used as focal points and as devices to emphasize perspective. And of course in Moorish and Islamic gardens water represents life itself and is central to the entire layout.

No matter what the style or size of the garden, water can be incorporated in some way. It could take the form of a simple wall fountain in a tiny rooftop garden, a birdbath in a shady corner, or an elegant water channel or rill running along the central axis of a large formal design.

In design, the most important factor when planning a water feature is to ensure that it is complementary to the overall mood and style of the garden. Another very important consideration is safety. If you are likely to have young children in the garden, ponds or pools near the house should be securely fenced or screened in some way.

In many areas water is a scarce commodity, and with rapidly expanding urban populations this is likely to be an ongoing problem. Therefore conservation is an important consideration when incorporating water in the garden. Where water supplies are low or there are extended dry periods, large water features may be inappropriate—a more modest feature, such as a fountain or small water trough, may be more suitable.

Contemporary gardeners and designers have some distinct advantages over those of the past. There is a vast choice of materials available, and modern technology also offers enormous scope for creativity in water features. At one end of the spectrum elaborate, often theatrical, special effects using water are made possible by computerized controls. And at the other, a simple bubble fountain where water bubbles up over a layer of pebbles, returning to a container below to be recycled, may be all that is needed.

RIGHT: The sharp lines of the white walls are perfectly balanced by the organic shape of the waterspout; the sound of trickling water over rocks completes the soothing effect.

BELOW: Water trickles down a glass wall into a pond, creating a serene atmosphere, ideal for contemplation.

OPPOSITE: A curved metal water wall adds a dynamic reflective element.

## FOUNTAINS

Fountains are particularly appealing because they are dynamic—they combine the soothing sounds and the visual appeal of moving water. The range of garden fountains available, whether for a tiny balcony or a rural property, is extensive, or you could create your own from whatever takes your fancy and suits the garden style.

Wall fountains are perfect for courtyards, creating a sense of privacy and sanctuary as well as bringing the space to life. For a classical garden, a stone or stone-look wall fountain is appealing, and for a very contemporary style, a stainless-steel spout over a simple trough of rendered cement is elegant.

Even tiny balconies can include a small fountain. There are many different bubble fountains available at nurseries which will fit easily into a ceramic pot or other container. Bell or dome fountains are particularly attractive in small spaces, as are simple but striking features such as water bubbling over a single large stone.

Dramatic effects can be achieved through the use of unusual materials and colors. Metal, glass and ceramics can all be used to create distinctive fountains, troughs and sculptural water features, as can recycled materials such as steel sheets and glass or plastic pipes. The orange wall with fountain on page 79 is a good example of how color and water can be combined to create a strong focal point and feature. A water wall, where the water falls in an unbroken sheet, can turn an otherwise static corner into a vibrant feature through its strong resemblance to a natural waterfall.

Fountains that have a number of different levels, or where water travels from one container to another, are very stimulating and often bring an extra element of sound to the garden. Water may pass from vessel to vessel, moving across a bed of pebbles, or it could set up a chain reaction so that bamboo strikes rhythmically against another piece of bamboo or stone.

TOP: This handmade water feature of beaten copper is brazed with silver and copper and is permanently weather resistant.

BOTTOM: Attractive slate tiles have been arranged in a spiral pattern to create a sculptural fountain.

OPPOSITE, CLOCKWISE FROM TOP LEFT: A small pond and fountain nestles into a lush corner; an ornate metal fountain creates a beautiful feature at the edge of a pond; watering cans have been artfully arranged to make a whimsical water feature; a sculpted copper waterlily sits partly submerged at the edge of a pond.

## PONDS AND REFLECTION POOLS

There is probably no other single garden feature that brings so much universal pleasure as a pond or pool. Still water brings tranquility and encourages relaxation and contemplation.

The type of pond will be dictated by the style of the garden. In a formal garden a regular geometric shape will work well, its lines echoing those of the house and the rest of the garden. Surrounding the pond you could use simple paving and edging such as limestone or sandstone or white gravel. For a more natural style, curved ponds may be edged with pebbles or slabs of rock arranged in an irregular pattern. In a minimalist garden a single slab of black granite flooded with a layer of water makes a stunning reflection pool.

With any pond or pool, however, it is important to retain the tranquil qualities. So while a trickle of water may enhance the atmosphere, a flamboyant cascade or fountain is best kept for more dramatic water features. Similarly, it is important not to overdo floating plants such as waterlilies; if they take over the whole surface, the pond will lose its reflective appeal.

BELOW LEFT: A moss-covered circular pond is accentuated by a raised pebble border.

BELOW RIGHT: A pebble and leaf installation dramatically enhances a concrete bench; leaves floating on the surface of the small rectangular pond cut into the end of the bench make a decorative display.

OPPOSITE: A charcoal bench with scarlet cushion overhangs a small oval pond, creating an interesting contrast of straight lines and organic shape.

Ponds also bring the pleasure of water plants and aquatic life such as fish and frogs to the garden. Waterlilies are the stars of the pond, putting forth sculptural flowers in many different shades from floating pads of heart-shaped leaves. Other floating plants include the water poppy, the yellow waterlily and the fringed waterlily. There is also a great range of marginal plants, such as ferns, arum lilies and irises, which thrive on the damp edges of ponds or in shallow water; alternatively, some marginals can be grown in containers and submerged at the water's edge.

To make a simple pond, dig a hole to the required depth and remove any sharp rocks. Line the hole with underlay and top this with flexible butyl pond liner. Allow an extra 7 inches (20 cm) of liner to overlap around the edges of the pond and then secure it with metal pegs. Edge the pond with rocks or pavers, covering the liner and pegs and overlapping the pond slightly. Finally, add water, aquatic plants and fish.

If you have small children using the garden, it is a good idea to put wire mesh over the pond, just below the surface of the water. If it is a dark color you will not notice it, particularly if plants are allowed to grow through it. The mesh will also protect fish from cats and birds.

TOP: This stone-edged pond with wooden jetty is in perfect harmony with the woodland setting.

BOTTOM: A pond provides the opportunity to add aquatic and marginal plants such as water lilies, irises, rushes and ferns.

OPPOSITE: This water lily-covered dam with its lush border of flowering marginals creates an idyllic setting. The same effect can be created on a smaller scale with a lily pond.

# WATER PLANTS AND MARGINALS

*Acorus calamus* (Sweet flag)—Ornamental reedlike perennials, these clump-forming marginal plants have scented sword-shaped leaves; there is also a cultivar with cream variegations.

*Caltha* species (Marsh marigold)—These classic marginal deciduous perennials have clusters of buttercuplike, bright golden-yellow flowers in spring.

*Hosta* species and cultivars (Plantain lily)—These elegant perennials like shady positions in moist soil, so are ideal for planting beside ponds. Their highly ornamental leaves, crimped and variegated in some types, are abundant in spring and die back in autumn. Many hostas also have clusters of trumpet-shaped flowers.

*Hydrocleys nymphoides* (Water poppy)—This water perennial prefers warm and temperate conditions. It has floating, rounded bright green leaves and dainty yellow poppylike flowers in summer.

*Iris* species and cultivars (Iris)—This extensive family of plants includes many species which grow in shallow water or pond margins, such as the yellow flag, *I. pseudacorus*; the blue flag, *I. versicolor*; the Siberian flag, *I. sibirica*; and the Japanese and Louisiana cultivars with their outstanding color range.

*Nuphar lutea* (Yellow waterlily)—Also commonly called brandy bottle, because of the unusual shape of the yellow flowers, this hardy perennial water plant has leathery floating leaves and is best in larger ponds.

*Nymphaea* species and cultivars (Waterlily)—This famous water plant has many varieties, with some that are hardy and others that require a tropical climate. *N.* 'Attraction' is a deciduous hardy perennial with cup-shaped, deep red flowers. Another hardy perennial, *N. marliacea* 'Albida' has white flowers that are highly fragrant. Blue-flowered waterlilies include the tropical species *N. capensis*, with star-shaped bright blue flowers, and the cultivar 'Blue Beauty', which has rounded deep blue flowers with striking yellow centers.

*Nymphoides peltata* (Fringed waterlily)—This hardy water perennial has floating, rounded leaves and bright yellow, fringed flowers throughout summer.

*Peltiphyllum peltatum* (Umbrella plant)—A marginal, spreading perennial with large umbrella-shaped leaves and clusters of pale pink flowers on tall stems in spring.

*Pontederia cordata* (Pickerel rush)—This deciduous perennial thrives in wet soil and marginal conditions with up to 12 inches (30 cm) of water. It has lance-shaped leaves with graceful architectural lines and spires of bright blue flowers in summer.

*Schoenoplectus lacustris* subsp. *tabernaemontani* 'Zebrinus' (Zebra rush)—This distinctively striped plant thrives in deeper marginal conditions; it can spread easily and needs to be kept under control by being cut back regularly.

OPPOSITE, CLOCKWISE FROM TOP LEFT: *Iris sibirica* (Siberian iris), with its sword-like leaves and bright purple flowers, is a hardy plant for pond margins; *Cyperus papyrus* is a very decorative water plant, its slender stems growing up to 3.1 m (10ft) and topped with feathery clusters of wiry spikes arranged in umbels; the sculptural shape of a water lily emerges from a bed of glossy green leaves; a wide range of plants are suitable for pond-side planting. Here, tufty Hakone grass (*Hakonechloa macra*) is combined with Japanese maple (*Acer palmatum*) and iris.

## CHANNELS AND RILLS

Channels and rills are narrow strips of still or moving water. In Islamic or Mogul gardens these were central features, running along the main axis of the garden and culminating in a fountain or raised platform. In formal gardens, both past and present, they serve the purpose of dividing the garden and leading the eye towards the horizon or a focal point.

In modern gardens, rills or channels are dynamic water features that can act as a miniature stream, perhaps traveling between a fountain and a pond, at the same time creating a strong sense of perspective.

A simple rill can be constructed of panels of toughened glass, stainless steel or even plastic piping. More elaborate channels and narrow canals can be constructed from stone or decorative tiles. Adding small stones or pebbles to the channel will create interesting patterns and soothing sounds as the water travels over them. It will also encourage people to bend down and touch them, as they are irresistibly tactile.

BELOW: A water rill runs through the middle of this formal terraced garden, culminating in a circular pond. Rills or channels are often used to create a strong sense of linear perspective, leading the eye to a focal point in the garden. In this case, a large tree is both reflected in the water channel and acts as a focal point.

OPPOSITE: A narrow rill dissects a cactus garden, the running water creating relief and balance to the dryness of the landscape and spiky forms of the plants.

## SWIMMING POOLS

A swimming pool can be an absolute delight, bringing hours of pleasure and relaxation, but it can also be a significant burden if not well planned. Before installing a swimming pool, it is important to carefully consider how much you will use it and how much time you can spare to maintain it. Another important consideration is water conservation, since water loss through evaporation is significant in swimming pools and they require regular top-ups. In many urban areas water restrictions, particularly during summer, may impact on pool maintenance.

If you do include a pool in your garden, the location and size are both major considerations. In many areas it is a requirement to have fencing around pools for the protection of young children, so if this is the case in your area it is important to allow enough space for the fence. However, enjoyment of the pool will be greatly diminished if people feel caged in while using it. You should also allow space for storage of pool equipment. Where space is limited, consider a smaller option such as a lap pool or a plunge pool.

The style of the pool needs to suit both the garden and the architecture of the house. A classic rectangular swimming pool is probably the best choice for most contemporary gardens, the shape complementing that of buildings and the garden itself. The color choice of the pool lining will impact dramatically on the mood it imparts and how it interacts with the rest of the garden. A dark blue or black lining makes a dramatic statement and maximizes reflection. This can work particularly well in a small contemporary courtyard, both aesthetically and in a design sense, as it has the effect of making the space seem larger. In a natural-style garden with abundant greenery, a pale green lining will take the eye beyond the pool to the similar hues of the foliage.

Paving around the pool area should match the paving in the rest of the garden, but make sure it is appropriate for poolside use. Alternatively, you can combine materials, such as paving tiles with a slate border, to provide surfaces that are safe and also reflect the garden's themes. Where there is plenty of sun, you can have a lawn almost to the edges of the pool—this can look wonderfully lush and inviting.

The plants that surround the pool will greatly enhance its theme. In a tropical setting, the pool can be nestled amongst palms and ferns, while in a Mediterranean-style garden tubs of orange and lemon trees would be the perfect complement. In contemporary gardens, architectural plants in dramatic containers make great poolside features. For a formal garden, clipped hedges will echo a pool's classic lines.

BELOW LEFT: This classic shaped pool works well in this formal garden. The soft hazy silver and mauve of the *Teucrium chamaedrys* hedge highlight the blue tones of the pool's tiles.

BELOW RIGHT: Dark tiling is a stylish backdrop to bright red geraniums and poolside chair and terracotta pots.

OPPOSITE: Water cascades into a swimming pool from the underneath edge of a beautifully crafted timber deck.

# Ornamentation

# ORNAMENTATION

The creation of focal points in the garden is the essence of good garden design. In nature, the physical landscape — mountains, lakes, rocks and beaches—provides focal points, as do outstanding plants such as large trees and brightly colored flowers and leaves. This variation in color, form and texture is deeply satisfying, and our eyes seek out these things when viewing landscape, both on the grand scale and in our own backyards.

In the garden, an ornament acts as a focal point that will always draw the eye, and bring a sense of order to a design. Ornaments—whether a fountain, pond, accent plant, sundial, urn, found object or cherished sculpture—also act as expressions of our personalities and styles, and provide a deeper level of meaning to the garden. However, it is the careful placement of these objects, rather than simply the ornaments themselves, that gives a garden distinction and makes it truly rewarding.

TOP: Metal seats with mauve painted timberwork turn a practical item into an enticing ornament in this small courtyard.

BOTTOM: A scarecrow adds a touch of whimsy and personality to a vegetable garden.

OPPOSITE, TOP LEFT: This delicate perspex mobile spins gently in the breeze.

OPPOSITE, TOP RIGHT: A glass dragonfly alights on some poolside sedge.

OPPOSITE, BOTTOM: Mirrors are useful devices to expand small areas. Here, a mirror on a rendered wall adds a new perspective, framing a reflected picture of the garden and wind chimes.

Using design devices effectively requires some understanding of the way the human eye views space and the importance of the rules of perspective. For example, we see parallel lines as converging in the distance, although in reality they do not. When looking at a garden, we look for outstanding objects or focal points of distinction that will help us assess distance and depth. We are drawn to the linear, both horizontal and vertical.

Renaissance designers displayed a sophisticated understanding of how to create focal points and vistas. Expansive views were given boundaries to scale them down and frame them, narrow spaces were made to appear wider, focal points were situated so as to draw the eye, and distance was distorted through the use of color and form.

The same rules are even more applicable in contemporary gardens, which generally have suburbia as a background. You can make use of the way the eye is constantly being led towards something to create a focal point, and divert attention from less visually appealing scenes. Linear structures and elements that attract and then direct the eye, such as alleys, avenues, borders and pathways, should be punctuated with focal points, as these keep the eye moving forward.

TOP: An avenue of medlars directs the view to a focal point where a large terracotta urn stands out against the green of the lawn and hedge background.

BOTTOM: A classic timber bench in the Jeckyll/Lutyens style is placed at the end of an impatiens-lined path.

OPPOSITE: A large decorative stone urn defines the focal point at the end of a gravel path lined with *Polygonium orientale*, *Cosmos* and *Verbena bonariensis*.

# DECORATIVE CONTAINERS AND URNS

Containers and urns can be used as decorative items in their own right or as vessels to display plants. Urns are a traditional form of garden decoration and were particularly popular in the eighteenth and early nineteenth centuries, when they were first mass produced. Many of those available today are reproductions of these Victorian and Edwardian urns and they work particularly well when matched with architecture of the same era. If your house is a modern one, however, it is probably more appropriate to look for materials and styles that match the building. For example, in urban formal courtyards, large terracotta or galvanized iron containers in simple geometric shapes look very effective; willow-weave planters fit well into a rustic kitchen garden.

Urns are designed to be placed above the ground, such as on a plinth, on gate piers, or in alcoves or niches. Some have lids and are purely ornamental, while others make great planting containers. Plants that gently cascade down the sides of an urn have a particular charm and accentuate the elegant lines of the container, but make sure the plant you select is reasonably tough, as watering may be less than ideal if the urn is located in an inaccessible location.

If placing an urn on a plinth, choose materials for the plinth that match or are complementary to the urn—the focus should be on the urn. The plinth should be firmly secured on a solid base. If it is placed on a paved or gravel surface, you can soften the lines by planting around the base. Soft, feathery groundcover plants such as seaside daisies or a hazy border of silvery-gray foliage like lavender are the perfect foils for the strong vertical lines of a plinth. For a more formal setting, box or other hedging sets off the plinth to great effect. Alternatively, place the plinth in a garden bed so that the urn rises above a sea of leaves and flowers.

ABOVE: A collection of terracotta pots, a metal bucket used as a planter and an old fashioned packing crate and watering can make an attractive eclectic display.

OPPOSITE, CLOCKWISE FROM TOP LEFT: A stone urn with cascading display of petunias and lobelia creates a romantic and graceful feature; this elegant terracotta urn placed on white gravel at the end of a pathway draws the eye; an urn on a pedestal is accentuated by trailing variegated ivy; a rustic terracotta pot nestles behind the greenery.

Pots or containers will fit into all sorts of garden designs and spaces—in and around beds, on hard surfaces, hanging from walls, and on balconies and windowsills—and the choice of styles is infinite. Large ornate pots make spectacular decorative features, but take care not to overdo it. Too many decorative items will distract rather than enhance the garden. It is important to select containers that are in scale with the whole garden, as well as with the particular location where they are to be placed.

Choose the largest container the space can take; this gives the plants plenty of room to develop roots and thus a greater chance of survival. Many containers dry out easily: mulch will also help survival rates by cutting down water evaporation. In very dry positions, it is useful to add some water-retaining crystals to the potting mix.

When choosing pots, look for those that highlight the plants rather than compete with them. Terracotta, stone or glazed ceramic allow the plants to be the primary focus, and reconstituted stone is available in many different colors and textures at significantly lower cost than stone. On the other hand, if the pot is the feature, choose an understated plant that emphasizes the container's design.

TOP: A purple-tipped *Echeveria* surrounded by large pebbles makes a striking display in glossy ceramic pot.

BOTTOM: The terracotta pot, succulents and rustic brick wall create a warm, textured combination.

OPPOSITE, CLOCKWISE FROM TOP LEFT: A richly tiered display of potted grass and vibrant *Skimmia*; these square metal pots are a stylish understated choice for a contemporary terrace; the verdigris finish on this copper planter is enhanced by the choice of plants – crimson tulips and forget-me-nots; the simplicity of these tall, slanted pots is emphasized by the sculptural form of lemongrass.

You don't need to limit yourself to traditional pot materials. Many imaginative gardeners have recycled unusual objects as planters to great effect. Old concrete laundry tubs, and the round "coppers" in which water for washing clothes used to be boiled, are good deep containers for plants and have a charm of their own. Concrete pipes make interesting containers and look striking with plants that have strong, distinctive form and color, such as tufted grass or cacti. Bathtubs, wine barrels and concrete troughs have long been put to good use as attractive planters.

Also take advantage of the infinite range of contemporary materials which can be used with great imagination in the garden. Metal, such as polished copper, aluminum, galvanized steel and iron, fits particularly well into urban and architectural gardens, and also combines well with other materials. Glass can also look dramatic, particularly when it allows a view of a plant's root system and textured layers of pebbles and soil; however, if using glass in areas where the temperatures regularly drop below freezing, you will need to line the container with Perspex to prevent it cracking. Of course, plastic is an infinitely versatile material, lightweight and durable, for stylish containers of all shapes and sizes.

BELOW: A seemingly haphazard collection of tiny terracotta pots atop a stick fence and old metal containers is an artful display of cottage nostalgia.
OPPOSITE: Recycled containers and a cane basket filled with pansies lend this entrance a quaint and homely air.

## SUNDIALS

Sundials are eye-catching garden features that are ideal as focal points, especially at the end of a pathway or in the center of a lawn or courtyard. Possibly the most ancient of scientific instruments, they are the earliest known method of time-keeping. So, as well as being decorative, they are satisfyingly practical and bring something of the past to our gardens.

The earliest sundials relied on the height of the sun in the sky to indicate the time according to the length of the shadow it cast. By the first century AD, it was discovered that by placing the pointer, or gnomon, parallel to the earth's axis, a shadow would be cast in the same direction at the same time every day of the year. However, it was not until the fourteenth century, after the invention of the compass, that this could be accurately achieved.

Sundials became particularly popular in the gardens of the wealthy in Medieval and Renaissance times and they were very ornate in design. They have remained popular as garden decorations and can suit any style—formal or informal, traditional or contemporary. Both wall-mounted or freestanding versions are available. The main considerations for the location are that the sundial must receive sun all day if it is to be of practical use, and it needs to be accessible so that it can be easily viewed.

TOP: An elegant sundial is given greater emphasis by a clipped *Buxus* border.

MIDDLE: This sundial is given greater access by placing it in the middle of a circular paved niche.

BOTTOM: A solid stone sundial sits in a sea of pink begonias at the junction of four gravel paths.

OPPOSITE: A stone sundial is just visible at the end of a gravel path with a perennial border of lavender, *Campanula*, foxgloves and roses.

## OBELISKS

Obelisks, with their tapering, geometric shapes, make elegant garden ornaments and are both functional and decorative. The pointed structure and small base make an obelisk perfect for introducing the vertical element to a small garden. Where there is more space, they can be strategically placed as focal points, such as at the end of a path or archway.

Available in timber, stone or metal, obelisks should be chosen to complement other materials used in the garden and the house. While stone obelisks are usually used on their own as ornamental features, and set into gravel or paving, those made from timber and metal can be placed in garden beds to support climbing plants. Timber obelisks add a light, romantic touch to a garden bed, and a finely wrought metal one can also have an airy, delicate appearance. A simple obelisk can be created by using three bamboo or metal poles as a support structure for climbers such as sweet peas, clematis or beans in a vegetable garden.

BELOW: A blue timber obelisk makes a dramatic contrast to the surrounding greenery.

## NICHES

Traditionally used to display urns or busts, wall niches bring a classical element to the garden and are very suitable for formal gardens. They are useful devices in small areas—despite being quite shallow, a niche gives the impression of depth. This can be further accentuated by lattice work or by coloring the recess in a darker shade than the wall, creating a trompe l'oeil effect. You can also carve a niche into a formal hedge to create a greater sense of depth in a small enclosed area.

To work effectively, the niche should be at eye level and, since you will be creating an eye-catching feature, it is important that the wall is an attractive one, whether rendered, painted or rustic. And while traditional ornaments will suit strongly formal or architectural designs, you can use your niche to display any ornament that suits your garden, such as a modern sculpture, quirky artwork, a simple bowl or a collection of pebbles.

BELOW: The elegant simplicity of a terracotta wall plaque works perfectly in this wall niche.

OPPOSITE: A mirrored obelisk adds an intriguing element, with its captured image of metal pots and stone.

## PAINTED ACCENTS

Painting is a simple and fast way to revitalize your garden and to highlight particular areas. Fences, walls, decorative containers and furniture can all be given a coat of paint and the effect can be as subtle or as dramatic as you wish.

An unattractive concrete or brick wall can be easily transformed into a feature by rendering or bagging and then painting. For a soft, weathered look in a Mediterranean-style garden, limewash, a lime-based coating, is particularly effective; it fades and weathers beautifully and is very low maintenance. Or, for a striking feature wall, select a hot color like bright pink or orange, such as the one on page 79.

Using a color wheel can help create the effect you want. Colors opposite each other on the wheel are contrasting though complementary, while those adjacent on the wheel are harmonious. A scheme which combines both contrasting and harmonious tones can work well. For example, a terracotta-colored wall partly covered with a glossy green climbing plant and mass-planted with lavender at its base has, paradoxically, a both stimulating and soothing effect.

BELOW: The soft cream of the painted door and window works beautifully with the pale pink and cream climbing roses, creating a romantic entrance to this cottage.

OPPOSITE, CLOCKWISE FROM TOP LEFT: This brightly painted seat and arbor is the ideal nook for an eye-catching stained glass panel; a blue painted pergola provides an attractive contrast to a Bougainvillea's showy scarlet flower bracts; blue planter boxes make a feature of these vegetable beds; table, chairs, watering can, doors and wall in this courtyard harmonize in different shades of blue.

An integrated color scheme pulls together different elements of the garden. A silver-gray foliage border, such as lamb's ear, can be picked up on a piece of garden furniture or a row of pots and then repeated on the door of a garden shed to create a sense of movement and integration. You can make the garden appear larger by using soft colors to blur the furthest boundary, or conversely you can shorten a long, narrow space by using vibrant colors in the foreground. To create the sense of more space on a narrow balcony, the hand rail and furniture can be painted in soft shades of green to echo the greenery of the garden, drawing the eye beyond the immediate area.

Colorful accents can also be created by painting ornaments in the same tones—try a group of pots, or an eclectic collection of old watering cans and tins. When selecting colors to use as accents, take into account the strength of the light where you live. Saturated colors like deep terracotta and bright blue or hot colors like magenta or shocking pink work well in hot climates, such as the Mediterranean, Australia, South Africa and Latin America, where the light is intense, while more muted tones are better suited to softer northern light.

TOP: A mauve retaining wall brings out the vivid pink of the *Prunus* blossoms and complements the dark green of the deep green foliage.

BOTTOM: Painting these rough wood planters in yellow and blue has imbued this vegetable plot with a cheerful, casual mood which is further enhanced by the brightness of the pink ivy geranium.

OPPOSITE: The stressed painted finish is perfect for this beautiful Asian water gate, creating a feeling of antiquity and providing a decorative frame for the rambling garden and ornate statue.

# SCULPTURE

Art and sculpture have long played a vital role in the garden. Japanese and Chinese gardens traditionally place much emphasis on the careful inclusion of sculptural elements, many of which are objects from nature such as rocks or trees. In Islamic gardens brilliantly colored wall murals depicted the gardens of Paradise that the earthly ones aspired to emulate, while the Romans added fine statuary and sculpture to the tradition of elaborate wall murals. Renaissance Europe saw a flourishing of sculpture commissioned for both public and private gardens, and many of these are still there for us to admire today.

We increasingly use sculpture to make statements about our environment and culture or simply for its aesthetic appeal. Sculpture has a powerful impact; it is tactile and three-dimensional and, like all art, has the potential to move us on levels other than the purely visual. The garden is a very sympathetic setting for sculpture, whether an artwork is positioned so that it emerges from its surrounds to create an element of surprise or placed as an attention-grabbing central feature.

BELOW LEFT: A striking sculpture of *Melia* stems is set against a purple wall.
BELOW RIGHT: A sculpted head with conifer 'hair' makes a powerful impact.
OPPOSITE: A serene stone Buddha sits underneath a Japanese maple (*Acer palmatum*) in a quiet corner of the garden.

Choosing sculpture for your garden is a very personal and subjective exercise. Depending on the style of your house and garden and the placement of the sculpture, you might select traditional statuary, an animal sculpture or an abstract piece made of metal, wood, stone or synthetic materials. Your budget will usually determine whether you have a one-off piece or an "off-the-shelf" sculpture. And while a specially created work of art will bring extra meaning to your garden as well as a lifetime of pleasure, so will a found object of great personal significance.

Statues have traditionally been associated with figures, usually human, but also mythological gods and creatures from our legends and stories. While in public gardens, statues are usually life-size or larger, in a domestic setting it is likely they will be considerably smaller. Statues are typically made from metal or stone, but it is also possible to buy cheaper representations made from resin combined with mineral aggregates. Only the most expensive items are now individually carved, the majority of mass-produced statues being cast in concrete or a combination of crushed stone and cement. Gardening magazines and garden centers are a good source for statues and sculpture. For an antique, you should try dealers and auction houses.

RIGHT: A circle of stones marks the boundary between forest and garden, its formation striking a balance between simple elegance and primitive art.

INSET TOP: A bronze statue rests gracefully in a grass garden, backed by a golden cloud of *Miscanthus sinensis* flower heads.

INSET MIDDLE: Pan nestles amongst a grapevine bower.

INSET BOTTOM: This sculpted head has an imposing presence in a perennial border.

Animal sculptures are popular for the garden, and they provide plenty of scope for creating amusing and whimsical scenes or to simply add a friendly element to a corner of the garden. While some gardeners love to succumb to the kitsch or sentimental when choosing an animal sculpture, others may opt for subtlety, such as pair of wiremesh guinea fowl in the vegetable garden or a carved wooden owl perched in a quiet corner.

Abstract sculpture, apart from really standing out in the garden, can also provide a great deal of personal meaning. These ornaments can include anything from a suggestive arrangement of found objects, or a simple placement of beautiful stones, to an elaborate creation of cast metal, plastic or glass. Driftwood found on a memorable holiday, old tree trunks and root burrs, or an ancient metal wheelbarrow could all feature in your garden.

TOP LEFT: A painted pole installation echoes the colors and shapes of the surrounding foliage.

TOP RIGHT: The incongruous placement of a metal bedhead creates an interesting focal point.

ABOVE: Placed objects, such as these beautiful stones, can be purely decorative or carry a deeper personal significance.

OPPOSITE, CLOCKWISE FROM TOP LEFT: As real as they may appear, these sculpted magpies, gathered around a large wooden pot, are not likely to fly away as you approach; a stone pig peers out from a bed of dainty aquilegias; a chorus of magpies perch on top of wooden poles in this whimsical sculpture; willow-weave deer add a friendly touch to a lawn.

## MOSAICS

Mosaics involve the creation of patterns with small pieces of colored or textured material embedded in cement. These patterns can be as simple or as complex as you want, and can be used as decorative features on walls, in paving or on items of outdoor furniture such as tables.

For inspiration, you can look to the wonderfully intricate patterns and vibrant colors of Moorish mosaics. Or for a more subtle approach, look at the Italian-style mosaics of Roman gardens, which are focused on variations in textures and more muted tones.

Commonly used materials for mosaics are small tiles of glass, marble, glazed ceramic or mirror, or broken or unevenly sized fragments of these materials. The materials which can be used in mosaic are infinite, and richly textured or colored patterns can be created using metal, shells, wood and even plastic.

OPPOSITE, FAR LEFT: Mosaic stepping stones with a simple fish motif make a highly decorative and tactile feature in this lawn.

OPPOSITE, TOP: An ornate mosaic pot adds a touch of the exotic to a formal garden, the richness of the colors and elaborate patterning contrasting dramatically with the plain green surrounds.

OPPOSITE, MIDDLE: Fragments of ceramic tiles have been used for this mosaic pattern on a step, the border created by setting pebbles in cement.

OPPOSITE, BOTTOM: This colorful mosaic pot and shelf have been created from unevenly sized pieces of broken patterned ceramic.

RIGHT: A richly patterned mosaic pot and a sculptural spiky succulent make a striking feature.

PAGE 198: A mirror attached to a painted trellis and draped with clematis suggests an opening in the fence with a view to another gravel courtyard – a useful device for creating a sense of greater space in a small garden.

PAGE 199: A small courtyard is visually extended through the skilful use of trompe l'oeil.

# TROMPE L'OEIL

Trompe l'oeil can be a very effective way of creating the illusion of more space or of a view beyond the garden. A French term literally meaning "trick the eye," trompe l'oeil is a style of painting which gives the appearance of three-dimensional, or photographic, realism. Very popular during the Renaissance, trompe l'oeil methods became even more sophisticated in fifteenth-century Italy as artists and designers began to explore linear perspective.

Tromp l'oeil can add a playful touch to your garden, allowing you to create whole new vistas and decorative features. You may like to have a view of mountains glimpsed through stone archways, or an avenue of trees leading to some meadows instead of a brick wall at the end of your garden. In small gardens, subtle and quirky trompe l'oeils can become memorable features—pots of flowers painted on a courtyard wall, or a window with your ideal outlook.

A false perspective can also be created using decorative trellis. Just as an artist would make use of linear perspective to draw a pathway leading off to the distance, so trellis can be arranged on walls to look like archways, tunnels and recesses, giving the impression that the garden continues beyond its immediate boundaries.

# Living
## in the Garden

# LIVING IN THE GARDEN

Spending time in your garden is a just reward for all the hard work of planning, creating and nurturing it. And whether for you this means planting and creating exciting designs, just relaxing and revitalizing removed from the everyday world, or entertaining and feeding the hordes, furnishing your garden is essential.

Somewhere to sit, eat or play makes your garden an extension of your home. For this, outdoor furniture such as benches and tables and protective structures such as shades and awnings are both practical and decorative. Lighting will also help maximize your enjoyment of the garden, bringing it to life at night and opening up completely new aspects of the space.

TOP: A decorative hanging seat made of metal and cane puts a large tree to good use and creates a relaxing spot to read, contemplate, or even have a nap.

BOTTOM: A wooden lounger maximizes a view of this pretty perennial border and is strategically located adjacent to the barbecue.

OPPOSITE: The style and type of garden furniture says a great deal about how the garden is used; this stylish cane lounger and two comfortable chairs instantly imbue this garden with a relaxed mood.

# GARDEN FURNITURE

Outdoor furniture such as tables, benches and awnings is both functional and decorative. There are many choices of materials for garden furniture—timber, stone, reconstituted stone, metal and plastic—in both traditional and contemporary styles. The furniture type you select will depend largely on the style of your garden and on how you intend to use it.

Timber and stone furniture is solid in appearance and brings a certain weightiness to the garden. Hardwood furniture such as teak, iroko and cedar is expensive but will last a lifetime—and it weathers beautifully, requiring little more than a coat of oil every few years. Take care that any hardwood furniture you purchase is made from plantation timber. Softwood furniture will need to be painted with a protective preservative and stored away during winter. It can also be painted to create a fresh look or to make a strong visual impact. Pastel shades and white can work particularly well with flowering perennial borders.

ABOVE: A cane seat and tiny pergola constructed of wooden poles makes a cozy nook.

BELOW LEFT: A favorite spot in the garden is the ideal place for a pretty metal and timber chair, its cheery red paintwork matching the color scheme of the flower beds.

BELOW RIGHT: This stone bench has been tucked into a peaceful, secluded corner.

Metal furniture varies dramatically in quality and appearance. Unfortunately, cheaply made cast metal furniture can be unattractive, as well as heavy, and does not do a great deal to enhance the garden. Good quality wrought metal furniture, both the antique and modern versions, is a better long-term investment and suits formal settings and romantic styles; it also lends itself to being painted. For a contemporary look, stainless steel and aluminum are economical, light and very low maintenance.

Resin, plastic and perspex are versatile materials for furniture. While cheap plastic is not the most stylish choice, it is handy for extra seats and tables. Perspex and resin are more durable, are very lightweight, and can be virtually transparent, making them perfect for elegant minimalist designs. Outdoor furniture that cleverly combines materials such as shiny steel and glass or recycled timber and iron is is increasingly available.

RIGHT: A white metal bench is the perfect choice for underneath this flowering pear tree (*Pyrus calleryana*).

BELOW LEFT: The transparency of perspex furniture, such as these loungers and small table, means it does not visually crowd a space.

BELOW RIGHT: This beautiful corner with cascading white rose is enhanced by an ornate metal chair.

## Seats and benches

Seats and benches are important garden features. Both practical and ornamental, they can be used as focal points or they can be tucked out of sight in a secluded, contemplative spot. Even when not in use, attractive seating adds to the mood of a garden, conjuring up images of relaxation or celebration. A poolside lounger, a hammock attached to a shady tree, and an elegant teak bench in a quiet corner create different images and associations but all represent important aspects of a garden's use.

Natural fibers and materials such as wicker, woven willow and timber are all very sympathetic for use in the garden. Simple and inexpensive timber seating such as deck chairs and folding canvas director's chairs can look very effective if you want to match fabrics to your outdoor décor. They are also portable and light and easily folded away for storage.

Built-in benches and seats, particularly where there are solid walls to attach them to, are useful in small gardens and courtyards and have a streamlined appearance. The seats can double as storage space so that cushions, gardening tools or fold-up stools can be put away when not in use. Custom-made seating can get around problems such as awkwardly shaped areas or tiny spaces, and also allow you to create individual and distinctive furniture. For small balconies or roof-top gardens, bench seating that folds up against a wall when not used is a space-saving solution.

Seating can be creatively simple, too. For example, a bench can be made using two large galvanized metal planters full of colorful plants to support a timber plank that is bolted to the sides of the planters. Logs and large pieces of driftwood can be fashioned into seats, and are especially effective in natural-style gardens. Low, wide retaining walls and steps can also double as seating, with specially made cushions making them even more inviting.

BELOW LEFT: A simply constructed wooden bench is ideal for this natural style garden.

BELOW RIGHT: Timber seats constructed around a tree have a distinctive charm.

OPPOSITE, CLOCKWISE FROM TOP LEFT: A moss-covered stone bench blends into a shady corner; this curved concrete bench with mosaic decorations has a New Mexico flavor; a hammock is the ultimate for relaxation.

## Outdoor dining furniture

Eating outdoors is one of life's true pleasures, and the concept of the outdoor dining room is increasingly popular. While alfresco dining has long been an established part of the lifestyle in temperate climates such as the Mediterranean, Latin America and Australia, modern furnishings, protective awnings and portable outdoor heating can now make it a reality for those living in cooler northern climates as well.

In fact outdoor living and dining are now so firmly entrenched that for many people the selection of an outdoor dining setting is just as important as the selection of the indoor one. When choosing your outdoor dining furniture, take into account the size, style and usage patterns of your garden. There is little point investing in a bulky dining setting to accommodate large numbers of people if you entertain only a few times each year. You would be much better off to have a couple of small permanent pieces to be enjoyed year-round, or opt for an extendable table and extra fold-up seating for the occasions when you have additional visitors. Conversely, if you are an enthusiastic entertainer, it is important to allow adequate space and furniture to accommodate your guests comfortably.

TOP: Solid stone table and metal chairs lend a stately air to this outdoor pavilion.

ABOVE: Teak garden furniture weathers to a beautiful soft gray or can be oiled to retain its rich color. Here, a simple teak setting matches the casual mood of this tropical garden.

OPPOSITE: Timber benches have been custom-made for this stylish outdoor area. The striped cushions and bolsters give it a more permanent and comfortable atmosphere and accentuate the blue of the painted pergola. The lush lawn with timber inserts could almost be a carpet complete with runners.

If space is very limited, one option is to attach a hinged tabletop to a wall. Another is to place small matching tables in separate areas of the garden—this saves space and creates linked focal points—then join them together for dining occasions.

Metal is a good choice for outdoor tables and chairs for small gardens because it is light in appearance and weight and so can be easily moved around. While heavier-looking than metal, timber offers the flexibility of a wide range. A stone dining table is a permanent feature so it will need to be a very special selection. On the other hand, there are also many convenient combinations of metal, timber, plastic and glass, including fold-up options.

For outdoor dining, chairs need to look good, but not at the expense of comfort. Cushions will make a huge difference to metal or timber chairs. These can be removed and stored away when not in use, or left outside permanently if made from waterproofed canvas.

BELOW: This setting, with its plump blue cushions and umbrella canopy, is an enticing place to gather.

OPPOSITE: An elegant metal and stone dining setting is a permanent feature in this courtyard.

## Poolside furniture

Poolside furniture can enhance the experience of relaxing by the pool, but if overdone the garden can become cluttered and the visual effect of the pool may be lost. This is particularly a concern in a small garden where the pool dominates and clean uncluttered lines are important. Poolside furniture made of timber or wrought iron is not easily movable, whereas plastic and aluminum can be more readily folded and stored away.

Cushions, mattresses and other soft furnishings need to be covered in a hardy fabric that can tolerate sunlight, water, chlorine and salt. Pool umbrellas are essential in many areas for protection from the sun. These can be more permanent fixtures if you install sockets in paving so the umbrella can be locked in, but in the majority of instances it is better to be able to remove the umbrella and store it when not needed.

BELOW: A quick snooze after lunch wouldn't be out of the question here, the hammock conveniently located next to an attractive timber setting.

OPPOSITE, TOP: A lattice pergola extends the shaded area on the side of this country house.

OPPOSITE, BOTTOM: Strips of canvas provide a light and airy canopy for this stone-paved courtyard.

## SHADES AND AWNINGS

Shades and awnings have the dual purpose of providing protection from the weather and adding atmosphere to the garden by creating a sense of enclosure and shelter. They can be permanent or temporary structures, depending on the aspect of the garden and your particular requirements.

Permanent awnings are expensive but they can substantially increase the usage of outdoor areas, providing shelter from harsh midday sun and rain showers. These awnings are usually made from canvas; white or cream are the best colors for deflecting the sun and providing a cooling effect.

Less permanent shades and awnings can be made from sections of muslin or shadecloth by slinging them between the wall of the house and a nearby tree, or between posts. These can provide temporary shade and a create a more intimate space, such as for a child's sandpit or a balcony dining area.

## LIGHTING

The garden is transformed into a vastly different world at night—trees appear taller and closer, sounds are more apparent, ponds look dark and mysterious, shadows leap and dart, and the world beyond the garden disappears. Lighting can enhance the sensual atmosphere of the night garden, bringing to life certain areas and features and adding a soft glow to the structural elements.

Installing a well-planned and integrated lighting system is a wise investment. Apart from being practical, lighting will dramatically increase the time you are able to spend in the garden, as well as your enjoyment of it. When planning your garden lighting, whether it's a simple but effective row of flares or an elaborate light display, you will need to decide what features you want to emphasize and what sort of mood you want to evoke.

BELOW: Strategically placed up lights in this stylized white-washed courtyard create a shadow play and emphasize the curved metal water feature.

OPPOSITE: Candles are a romantic addition to this vine-covered arbor, providing soft lighting for night dining.

These days, there's a great range of garden lighting products available, to create all sorts of effects. One of the first decisions you will need to make is whether to use low voltage or mains voltage for your garden lighting. There's a wide selection of low-voltage lighting options now available, and these are designed to be easily and safely installed by the home-gardener. The smaller size of low-voltage light fittings also means they are easier to incorporate into a design or to conceal. If you decide to use mains voltage, you must have the lighting installed by a qualified electrician. If you're planning an elaborate light show in your garden, it is worthwhile consulting an outdoor lighting expert.

There are two distinctly different purposes for garden lighting—for practicality and for decoration. Practical lights include those for safety and security, and these are most commonly used in areas close to the house. Usually operated by sensors, they will flood an area with bright light. This is important for practical purposes but not compatible with decorative lighting, which aims to create atmosphere, so it is a good idea to have the two types of lighting on separate circuits, allowing you to operate the systems independently.

## OUTDOOR LIGHTING STYLES

The most common natural source of artificial light—the candle—is often the most effective in the garden. It is soft and romantic and readily available. For outdoor eating, candles on the dining table are hard to beat. Glass shades and lanterns protect the flame from blowing out and will accentuate the light. Rows of large outdoor candles can be used to edge pathways or to highlight features such as sculptures or topiary. Flares on bamboo or metal poles are also dramatic along a pathway, lighting the way for guests. An added advantage of candles and flares is that they are available with insect repellent, usually citronella based.

Downlights and uplights create very different effects. Downlights are useful for lighting outdoor dining tables or special features such as sculptures. When shining down from a height such as a tall tree, they can suggest moonlight and create some interesting shadow-play.

Uplights come in many different styles and are used to illuminate feature plants, pathways, steps, pools, ornamental ponds and fountains. Wonderful shadow effects can be created by placing uplights at the base of a wall, a sculpture or tree. Height can be emphasized and shapes accentuated, depending on the placement of the light. Experiment with the different effects by moving the lights around.

RIGHT: A galvanized metal light tower with fibre optic lights behind small glass windows makes an interesting feature, casting a muted light onto the nearby table.

OPPOSITE, CLOCKWISE FROM TOP LEFT: A glass platform in this courtyard is lit at night by panels of tiny lights. Behind, the white walls and a stand of bamboo are washed with light from two spotlights, while a sculptural light feature illuminates a staircase; a glass and metal lamp highlights a feature plant; glass benches and table are bathed in an ethereal glow from the garden beds below; a simple lantern with candle attached to a timber pergola is perfect for a romantic atmosphere.

Spotlights are particularly effective for emphasizing sculptures, water features and accent plants, as they can be tilted at different angles and directions. Take care, though, as they can flatten surfaces, removing the element of mystery or the interplay of light and shade if overused or placed too close to the object. Spotlights are available as wall mounts or on movable spikes that push into the ground.

Post lights are ideal for lighting pathways and can look very stylish when used for entrances. They are available in many different styles but a minimalist look in plain black or chrome is particularly effective, the glow of the light rather than the detailing being the main focus.

Pinpoints of light such as fairy lights strung in a tree add a magical touch. A similar effect is offered by fiber optics, with the light passing through strands of glass fiber to make tiny dots of light. Lanterns and other hanging lights also have a romantic appeal.

Underwater lighting has a dramatic effect. It brings a theatrical atmosphere to water features and emphasizes the movement and transparency of water. Pools dotted with underwater wall lights become inviting and mysterious, waterfalls lit from behind or below seem more dramatic, and ornamental ponds become a stage for dancing insects and rippling light.

TOP: Dots of light cast an electric blue glow in this highly stylized pond, strongly emphasizing the sculptural form of the potted Agave.

ABOVE: A simple lantern-style wall light enhances a vine-covered wall.

OPPOSITE: Underwater lighting adds a touch of theatre to this courtyard, throwing an eery glow onto the lion wall fountain.

# INDEX

# ACKNOWLEDGMENTS

The photographer would like to thank the following for their kindness in allowing their gardens to be photographed.

## Cover

Fiona Harrison, cover top right; Cullity Taylor, cover middle far left, back cover far left; Mark Vowles, cover bottom; Karla Newell, back cover 3rd from top; Hannath garden, back cover bottom

## Designers

Acres Wild, UK: 22, 68 left, 77 bottom, 113 bottom, 166

Allison Armour-Wilson, UK(artist): 205 bottom left

David Baptiste, Australia: 57 top left

Colin Blanche, Australia: 54 bottom left

Bold Simplicity, Australia: 49 top right

Humphrey Bowden, UK: 158 top, 159 bottom left

Michael Cooke, Australia: 37 top and bottom, 140 bottom right, 143, 144 bottom left, 169 bottom left, 192 top, 213 bottom

Cullity Taylor Design, Australia: 53 top, 76 top right, 93, 160 right, 161, 170

Andrew Duff, UK: 79

Rick Eckersley, Australia: 52 top

Christine Elsbury, Australia: 122 top right

Faulkner and Chapman, Australia: 17, 53 bottom left, 69, 169 bottom right

Jim Fogarty Design, Australia: 6 left, 51, 199 (artist Jim Blackie), 208

Fletcher and Myburgh, UK: 202 top

Peter Fudge, Australia: 67 bottom, 84 right, 97, 174 bottom

Harris Hobbs Landscapes, Australia: 188 top

Fiona Harrison, UK: 15, 74 top, 85 right, 86, 157 top

Maggy Howarth/Erik de Maeijer/Jane Hudson, UK: 4/5, 64

Lucy Huntington, UK: 3, 57 bottom right

Inside Out Urban Garden Design, Australia: 158 bottom, 179 top right and bottom left, 211

Sue Isherwood, Australia: 196 left

Japanese Garden Society, UK: 41

Katisma Landscaping, Australia: 168, 212

Die Landschafts Architekten, Germany: 75 bottom

Living Exteriors, Australia: 9

Darryl Mappin, Australia: 73, 132 bottom

Cherry Mills Garden Design, UK: 42 top left

Sue Montgomery, Australia: 14 (artist Yolande Oakley)

Sarah Morgan, UK: 40 top left

Andrew Muggeridge, UK: 110 top

Philip Nash, UK: 13 top left, 76 bottom left, 116 right, 156, 157 bottom, 214, 216 top left and bottom right, 218 top

Eileen Newell, UK (sculptor): 192 bottom

Karla Newell, UK: 12, 44, 46, 47 right, 80, 172 top, 195 bottom right, 220

Pickard School of Garden Design, UK: 54 top right

Pockett Wilson, UK: 10/11, 13 bottom right

Gaye Porter, Australia (sculptor): 193

Miriam Porter (sculptor): 194 top left, bottom right

Rock n' Root, Australia: 50, 207 top right

Penny Rudduck, Australia: 173 bottom

Secret Gardens of Sydney, Australia: 55 bottom, 84 left

Susan Sharkey, UK: 119

Small Wood Design, UK: 53 bottom right, 189

Gillian Temple, UK: 16

Theories Landscapes, UK: 48 bottom, 133 top, 217

Twisted Smiths, Australia: 159 top right

Mark Vowles, Australia: 6 bottom right, 209 bottom

Webb Landscapes, Australia: 147 top

Gay Wilson, UK: 160 left

## Locations/Garden Owners

Amberley Castle, UK: 120 top

Architectural Plants, UK: 38 bottom, 114 first and second top, 121

Bankton Cottage, UK: 81 top middle, 126, 176 bottom left

Bonython Garden, UK: 37 middle

La Bouscarella, France: 162 top

Buchanan garden, Australia: 186 top right, 195 left

Bury Court, UK: 77 top (Piet Oudolf Design), 78 (Christopher Bradley-Hole design)

Carson garden, Canada: 47 left

La Casella, France: 20 bottom right, 24, 33 top left, 49 bottom, 96 top right, 100 right, 142 top right

Chenies Manor, UK: 33 top right, bottom left, 62 top

Chinthurst, UK: 7

Barbara Clare's garden, Australia: 90 top, 177, 195 top right, 213 top

Le Clos du Peyronnet, France: 101

Compton Acres, UK: 39

Coverwood Lakes, UK: 100 left

Culverkeys, UK: 191 bottom right, 204 right

Dunsborough Park, UK: 20 bottom left

Five Oaks Cottage, UK: 181

Four Aces, UK: 26, 107, 109, 110 bottom, 182

The Garden Vineyard, Australia: 48 top

Hannath garden, UK: 58 bottom left, 192 middle

Hampton Cottage, UK: 180

Hatherways, UK: 54 top left

Heathside, UK: 176 top left, 183 bottom

Hemmant garden, UK: 13 bottom left, 27 bottom, 146, 205 bottom right

Hole Park, UK: 34 bottom left

Houghton Lodge, UK: 122 bottom left

Kennerton Green, Australia: 96 top left

Kingcups, UK: 45 bottom right, 67 top, 71 top, 75 top, 87 middle, 111 bottom

Lady Farm, UK: 32 top right, 90 bottom, 92

Lambley Nursery, Australia: 13 top right, 91, 140 top left, 194 bottom right

Larkins Farm, UK: 174 top

Latchetts, UK: 185, 186 top left, 188 bottom

Laurenden Forstal, UK: 82, 183 top

Long Barton, UK: 59

Longer End Cottage, UK: 27 top, 99 middle, 105 bottom, 108 bottom, 131

Meadow Cottage, UK: 172 bottom, 204 bottom left

Merriments, UK: 175

Moleshill, UK: 98, 118 bottom left, 120 bottom, 127, 179 top left, 186 bottom, 202 bottom

The Mosaic Garden, Australia: 53 bottom middle, 196 bottom right, 197

Old Place Farm, UK: 25, 28, 58 top right, 62 bottom left, 96 bottom left, 99 top, 112, 118 top left, 150, 176 bottom right

Parham House gardens, UK: 31, 76 bottom right

Park Terrace, UK: 187, 215

Periteau House, UK: 87 bottom

Pondokkie, Australia: 159 top left

Red Cow Farm, Australia: 66, 71 bottom

Reverie, Australia: 167

Sands, UK: 147 bottom

Selehurst, UK: 104 top

Sparrowhatch, UK: 124, 152 top, 194 bottom left

Special Plants, UK: 132 top, 140 bottom left, 203

Spring Cottage, UK: 40 top right, 102, 105 top, 183 middle

Stratford House, Australia: 200

Thyme Square, New Zealand: 72

Tilford Cottage, UK: 40 bottom left, 60, 61 second top, 68 right

Tillingbourne, UK: 159 bottom right

Town Place, UK: 18, 61 bottom, 103, 111 top, 118 bottom right

Turn End, UK: 19, 63

Vale End, UK: 125

Villa Parma, Australia: 21, 23, 70, 196 top right

West Dean College, UK: 122 bottom right, 152 bottom

West Dean Garden, UK: 176 top right, 190, 207 bottom

Whitehouse Cottage, UK: 20 top right, 63 bottom right

Wigandia, Australia: 57 bottom left

Wilson's Mill, New Zealand: 163

Woodbury Cottage, UK: 29, 57 top right, 74 bottom, 133 bottom, 140 top right, 162 bottom

Yalding Organic Gardens, UK: 30, 54 bottom right, 99 bottom